COLLINS GEM

GERMAN
GRAMMAR

COLLINS
GEM

GERMAN GRAMMAR

**Ilse McLean
Lorna Sinclair**

**Collins
London and Glasgow**

First published 1985

ISBN 0 00 459335 9

© **William Collins Sons & Co. Ltd. 1985**

Printed in Great Britain by
Collins Clear-Type Press

INTRODUCTION

This book has been designed to help all learners of German to get to grips with the grammar of the language, whatever stage you are at in learning German. For beginners, the book provides a clear introduction to all the basic rules and structures, and more advanced learners will find it an invaluable guide for reference and revision.

For ease of use, each part of speech (nouns, verbs, adjectives etc) has been treated separately (see the list of contents on the next page). Wherever we think a grammatical term may be unfamiliar this has been explained or illustrated at the appropriate point in the text.

A special feature of this compact book is the clear demarcation of grammatical points, each treated on a left-hand page, and illustrated by examples in up-to-date German on the opposite right-hand page. The eye is guided instantly to the appropriate example(s) by a system of bracketed numbers, e.g. (→1), (→2) etc, corresponding to an example number on the facing page. This means a clear, uncluttered presentation of the grammatical points, while allowing plenty of space for illustrating them.

Particular attention is paid throughout to those areas where German usage differs from English, thus helping the user to avoid the pitfalls of translating English structures by identical structures in German. Further sections at the back of the book give guidance in the use of numbers, and an area where German is very different from English: punctuation.

A fully comprehensive index, listing key words in both English and German, as well as grammatical references, completes the book.

Abbreviations used

acc.	accusative	gen.	genitive
ctd.	continued	masc.	masculine
dat.	dative	neut.	neuter
fem.	feminine	nom.	nominative
ff.	and following pages	p(p).	page(s)

4 CONTENTS

6 VERBS

Tense Formation

Tenses are either **simple** or **compound**. Once you know how to form the past participle, compound tenses are similar for all verbs (see pp.22 to 29). To form simple tenses you need to know whether a verb is **weak, strong** or **mixed**.

Simple Tenses

In German these are:

Present indicative   (→**1**)
Imperfect indicative   (→**2**)
Present subjunctive   (→**3**)
Imperfect subjunctive (→**4**)

Subjunctive forms are widely used in German, especially for indirect or reported speech (see pp.66 and 67).

The simple tenses are formed by adding endings to a verb **stem**. The endings show the number, person and tense of the subject of the verb (→**5**)

The types of verb you need to know to form simple tenses are:

● **Strong verbs** (pp.12 to 15), those whose vowel usually changes in forming the imperfect indicative (→**6**)

● **Weak verbs** (pp.8 to 11), which are usually completely regular and have no vowel changes. Their endings differ from those of strong verbs (→**7**)

● **Mixed verbs** (pp.16 and 17), which have a vowel change like strong verbs, but the endings of weak verbs (→**8**)

Continued

1 ich hole
I fetch, I am fetching, I do fetch

2 ich holte
I fetched, I was fetching, I used to fetch

3 (daß) ich hole
(that) I fetch/I fetched

4 (daß) ich holte
(that) I fetched

5 ich hole   I fetch
   wir holen   we fetch
   du holtest   you fetched

6 singen   to sing
   er singt   he sings
   er sang   he sang

7 holen   to fetch
   er holt   he fetches
   er holte   he fetched

8 nennen   to name
   er nennt   he names
   er nannte   he named

Weak Verbs

Weak verbs are usually **regular** in conjugation. Their simple
tenses are formed as follows:

- **Present** and **imperfect** tenses are formed by adding the
  endings shown below to the verb **stem**. This stem is
  formed by removing the **-en** ending of the infinitive (the
  form found in the dictionary) (→**1**)

- Where the infinitive of a weak verb ends in **-eln** or **-ern**,
  only the **-n** is removed to form the verb stem (→**2**)

- The endings are as follows (→**3**):

	PRESENT INDICATIVE	PRESENT SUBJUNCTIVE
1st. singular	**-e**	**-e**
2nd.	**-st**	**-est**
3rd.	**-t**	**-e**
1st. plural	**-en**	**-en**
2nd.	**-t**	**-et**
3rd.	**-en**	**-en**

	IMPERFECT INDICATIVE	IMPERFECT SUBJUNCTIVE
1st. singular	**-te**	**-te**
2nd.	**-test**	**-test**
3rd.	**-te**	**-te**
1st. plural	**-ten**	**-ten**
2nd.	**-tet**	**-tet**
3rd.	**-ten**	**-ten**

Continued

1 INFINITIVE   STEM

holen	to fetch	**hol-**
machen	to make	**mach-**
kauen	to chew	**kau-**

2

wandern	to roam	**wander-**
handeln	to trade, to act	**handel-**

3 **holen**   to fetch

PRESENT INDICATIVE	PRESENT SUBJUNCTIVE	
ich hole	ich hole	I fetch
du holst	du holest	you fetch
er/sie/es holt	er/sie/es hole	he/she/it fetches
wir holen	wir holen	we fetch
ihr holt	ihr holet	you (*plural*) fetch
sie/Sie holen	sie/Sie holen	they/you (*polite*) fetch

IMPERFECT INDICATIVE AND SUBJUNCTIVE
(*These tenses are identical for weak verbs*)

ich holte	I fetched
du holtest	you fetched
er/sie/es holte	he/she/it fetched
wir holten	we fetched
ihr holtet	you (*plural*) fetched
sie/Sie holten	they/you (*polite*) fetched

Weak Verbs (ctd.)

- Where the stem of a weak verb ends in **-d** or **-t**, an extra **-e-** is inserted before those endings where this will ease pronunciation (→**1**)

- Weak verbs whose stems end in **-m** or **-n** may take this extra **-e-**, or not, depending on whether its addition is necessary for pronunciation. If the **-m** or **-n** is preceded by a consonant *other than* **l**, **r** or **h**, the **-e-** is inserted (→**2**)

- Weak (and strong) verbs whose stem ends in a sibilant sound (**-s**, **-z**, **-ß**) normally lose the **-s-** of the second person singular ending (the **du** form) in the present indicative (→**3**)

NOTE: When this sibilant is **-sch**, the **-s-** of the ending remains (→**4**)

1 reden to speak

PRESENT	IMPERFECT
ich rede	ich redete
du redest	du redetest
er redet	er redete
wir reden	wir redeten
ihr redet	ihr redetet
sie reden	sie redeten

arbeiten to work

PRESENT	IMPERFECT
ich arbeite	ich arbeitete
du arbeitest	du arbeitetest
er arbeitet	er arbeitete
wir arbeiten	wir arbeiteten
ihr arbeitet	ihr arbeitetet
sie arbeiten	sie arbeiteten

2 atmen to breathe

PRESENT	IMPERFECT
ich atme	ich atmete
du atmest	du atmetest
er atmet	er atmete
wir atmen	wir atmeten
ihr atmet	ihr atmetet
sie atmen	sie atmeten

segnen to bless

PRESENT	IMPERFECT
ich segne	ich segnete
du segnest	du segnetest
er segnet	er segnete
wir segnen	wir segneten
ihr segnet	ihr segnetet
sie segnen	sie segneten

BUT:

umarmen to embrace

ich umarme	ich umarmte
du umarmst	du umarmtest
er umarmt	er umarmte
wir umarmen	wir umarmten
ihr umarmt	ihr umarmtet
sie umarmen	sie umarmten

lernen to learn

ich lerne	ich lernte
du lernst	du lerntest
er lernt	er lernte
wir lernen	wir lernten
ihr lernt	ihr lerntet
sie lernen	sie lernten

3 grüßen to greet

PRESENT
ich grüße
du grüßt
er grüßt
wir grüßen
ihr grüßt
sie grüßen

4 löschen to extinguish

PRESENT
ich lösche
du löschst
er löscht
wir löschen
ihr löscht
sie löschen

Strong Verbs

A list of the most useful strong verbs is given on pp.86 to 97.

- What differentiates strong verbs from weak ones is that when forming their **imperfect indicative** tense, strong verbs undergo a vowel change and have a different set of endings (→**1**)

  Their past participles are also formed differently (see p.24).

- To form the **imperfect subjunctive** of strong verbs, the endings from the appropriate table below are added to the stem of the imperfect indicative, but the vowel is modified by an umlaut where this is possible, i.e. **a → ä, o → ö, u → ü**. Exceptions to this are clearly shown in the table of strong verbs (→**2**)

The endings for the simple tenses of strong verbs are as follows (→**3**)

	PRESENT INDICATIVE	PRESENT SUBJUNCTIVE
1st. singular	**-e**	**-e**
2nd.	**-st**	**-est**
3rd.	**-t**	**-e**
1st. plural	**-en**	**-en**
2nd.	**-t**	**-et**
3rd.	**-en**	**-en**
	IMPERFECT INDICATIVE	IMPERFECT SUBJUNCTIVE
1st. singular	—	**-e**
2nd.	**-st**	**-(e)st**
3rd.	—	**-e**
1st. plural	**-en**	**-en**
2nd.	**-t**	**-(e)t**
3rd.	**-en**	**-en**

Continued

1 Compare:

	INFINITIVE	PRESENT	IMPERFECT
WEAK	**sagen** to say	er **sagt**	er **sagte**
STRONG	**rufen** to shout	er **ruft**	er **rief**

2

IMPERFECT INDICATIVE	IMPERFECT SUBJUNCTIVE
er **gab** he gave	er **gäbe** (*umlaut added*)
BUT er **rief** he shouted	er **riefe** (*no umlaut possible*)

3 singen to sing

PRESENT INDICATIVE	PRESENT SUBJUNCTIVE
ich sing**e**	ich sing**e**
du sing**st**	du sing**est**
er sing**t**	er sing**e**
wir sing**en**	wir sing**en**
ihr sing**t**	ihr sing**et**
sie sing**en**	sie sing**en**
Sie sing**en**	Sie sing**en**

IMPERFECT INDICATIVE	IMPERFECT SUBJUNCTIVE
ich sang	ich säng**e**
du sang**st**	du säng**(e)st**
er sang	er säng**e**
wir sang**en**	wir säng**en**
ihr sang**t**	ihr säng**(e)t**
sie sang**en**	sie säng**en**
Sie sang**en**	Sie säng**en**

Strong Verbs (ctd.)

- In the present tense of strong verbs, the vowel also often changes for the second and third persons singular (the **du** and **er/sie/es** forms).
  The pattern of possible changes is as follows:

  long **e** → **ie**
  short **e** → **i**
  a → **ä**
  au → **äu**
  o → **ö**

  Verbs which undergo these changes are clearly shown in the table on p.86 (**→1**)

- Strong (and weak) verbs whose stem ends with a sibilant sound (**-s**, **-z**, **-ß**) normally lose the **-s-** of the second person singular ending (the **du** form) in the *present indicative*, unless the sibilant is **-sch**, when it remains (**→2**)

- In the second person singular of the *imperfect* tense of strong verbs whose stem ends in a sibilant sound (including **-sch**) the sibilant remains, and an **-e-** is inserted between it and the appropriate ending (**→3**)

1 **sehen** to see   **helfen** to help
       ich sehe   ich helfe
       du **siehst**   du **hilfst**
       er/sie/es **sieht** er/sie/es **hilft**
       wir sehen   wir helfen
       ihr seht   ihr helft
       sie sehen   sie helfen

       fahren to drive   **saufen** to booze   **stoßen** to push
       ich fahre   ich saufe   ich stoße
       du **fährst**   du **säufst**   du stößt
       er **fährt**   er **säuft**   er stößt
       wir fahren   wir saufen   wir stoßen
       ihr fahrt   ihr sauft   ihr stoßt
       sie fahren   sie saufen   sie stoßen

2 **wachsen** to grow   **waschen** to wash
       ich wachse   ich wasche
       du **wächst**   du **wäschst**
       er **wächst**   er **wäscht**
       wir wachsen   wir waschen
       ihr wachst   ihr wascht
       sie wachsen   sie waschen

3 **lesen** to read   **schließen** to close   **waschen** to wash
       ich las   ich schloß   ich wusch
       du lasest   du schlossest   du wuschest
       er las   er schloß   er wusch
       wir lasen   wir schlossen   wir wuschen
       ihr last   ihr schloßt   ihr wuscht
       sie lasen   sie schlossen   sie wuschen

Mixed Verbs

There are nine **mixed** verbs in German, and, as their name implies, they are formed according to a mixture of the rules already outlined for weak and strong verbs.

The mixed verbs are:

denken to think   **kennen** to know   **nennen** to name
rennen to run   **senden** to send   **bringen** to bring
brennen to burn   **wenden** to turn   **wissen** to know

Full details of their principal parts are given in the verb list beginning on p.86.

- Mixed verbs form their **imperfect** tense by adding the weak verb endings to a stem whose vowel has been changed as for a strong verb (→**1**)

   NOTE: **bringen** and **denken** have a consonant change too in their imperfect forms (→**2**)

- The **imperfect subjunctive** forms of mixed verbs are unusual and should be noted (→**3**)

- Other tenses of mixed verbs are formed as for strong verbs.

- The past participle of mixed verbs has characteristics of both weak and strong verbs, as shown on p.24.

1 IMPERFECT INDICATIVE

kennen to know	**wissen** to know	**senden** to send
ich kannte	ich wußte	ich sandte
du kanntest	du wußtest	du sandtest
er kannte	er wußte	er sandte
wir kannten	wir wußten	wir sandten
ihr kanntet	ihr wußtet	ihr sandtet
sie kannten	sie wußten	sie sandten

2 IMPERFECT INDICATIVE

denken to think	**bringen** to bring
ich dachte	ich brachte
du dachtest	du brachtest
er dachte	er brachte
wir dachten	wir brachten
ihr dachtet	ihr brachtet
sie dachten	sie brachten

3 IMPERFECT SUBJUNCTIVE

kennen	**rennen**	**senden**
ich kennte	ich rennte	ich sendete
du kenntest	du renntest	du sendetest
er kennte *etc*	er rennte *etc*	er sendete *etc*

brennen	**wissen**	**wenden**
ich brennte	ich wüßte	ich wendete
du brenntest	du wüßtest	du wendetest
er brennte *etc*	er wüßte *etc*	er wendete *etc*

denken	**bringen**	**nennen**
ich dächte	ich brächte	ich nennte
du dächtest	du brächtest	du nenntest
er dächte *etc*	er brächte *etc*	er nennte *etc*

The Imperative

This is the form of a verb used to give an order or a command, or to make a request:

> *Come here/stand up/please bring me a beer*   (→1)

- German has three main imperative forms. These go with the three ways of addressing people **Sie, du** and **ihr** (see p.160)

	FORMATION	EXAMPLES	
SINGULAR	stem(+e)	hol(e)!	*fetch!*
PLURAL	stem+t	holt!	*fetch!*
POLITE (*sing* and *pl*)	stem+en Sie	holen Sie!	*fetch!*

- The **-e** of the singular form is often dropped, BUT NOT where the verb stem ends in **-t, -d, -chn, -ckn, -dn, -fn, -gn** or **-tm** (→2)

- **Weak verbs** ending in **-eln** or **-ern** take the **-e** ending in the singular form, but the additional **-e-** within the stem may be dropped (→3)

- Any vowel change in the present tense of a **strong verb** (see p.14) occurs also in its singular imperative form and no **-e** is added (→4)

  BUT if the vowel modification in the present tense of a **strong verb** is the addition of an umlaut, this is not added in the singular form of the imperative (→5)

- In the imperative form of a **reflexive verb** (see p.30) the pronoun is placed immediately after the verb (→6)

- **Separable prefixes** (see p.72) are placed at the end of an imperative statement (→7)

Continued

1 SINGULAR: **Komm mal her!**   Come here!
  PLURAL: **Steht auf!**   Stand up!
  POLITE: **Kommen Sie herein** Do come in

2 **Hör zu!** Listen
  Hol es! Fetch it
  BUT:
  Arbeite tüchtig! Work hard

3 **wandern**   to walk   **handeln**   to act
  wand(e)re! walk!   **hand(e)le!** act!

4 **nehmen**   to take   **helfen**   to help
  du nimmst you take   **du hilfst** you help
  nimm!   take!   **hilf!**   help!

  EXCEPTION:
  sehen   to see
  sieh(e)! see!

5 **laufen**   to run   **stoßen**   to push
  du läufst you run   **du stößt** you push
  lauf(e)!   run!   **stoß(e)!** push!

6 **sich setzen** to sit down:
  setz dich!
  setzt euch!
  setzen Sie sich!

7 **zumachen** to close: **aufhören** to stop:
  Mach die Tür zu!   **Hör aber endlich auf!**
  Close the door!   Do stop it!

The Imperative (ctd.)

● Imperatives are followed in German by an exclamation mark, unless the imperative is not intended as a command (→**1**)

● **du** and **ihr**, though not normally present in imperative forms, may be included for emphasis (→**2**)

● An imperative form also exists for the **wir** form of the verb. It consists of the normal present tense form, but with the pronoun **wir** *following* the verb. It is used for making suggestions (→**3**)

● The imperative forms of **sein** (*to be*) are irregular (→**4**)

● The particles **auch, nur, mal, doch** are frequently used with imperatives. They heighten or soften the imperative effect, or add a note of encouragement to a request or command. Often they have no direct equivalent in English and are therefore not always translated (→**5**)

Some Alternatives to the Imperative in German

● Infinitives are often used instead of the imperative in written instructions or public announcements (→**6**)

● The impersonal passive (see p.34) may be used (→**7**)

● Nouns, adjectives or adverbs can also be used with imperative effect (→**8**)
Some of these have become set expressions (→**9**)

1 Laß ihn in Ruhe! Leave him alone
Sagen Sie mir bitte, wie spät es ist
What's the time please?

2 Geht ihr voran! You go on ahead
Sag du ihm, was los ist You tell him what's wrong

3 Nehmen wir an also, daß ...
Let's assume then that ...
Sagen wir mal, es habe 4.000 DM gekostet
Let's just say it cost 4,000 marks

4 sein to be
sei!
seid!
seien wir!
seien Sie!

5 Geh doch! Go on!/Get going!
Sag mal, ... Tell me ...
Versuchen Sie es mal! Do give it a try!
Komm schon! Do come/Please come
Mach es auch richtig! Be sure to do it properly

6 Einsteigen!
All aboard!
Zwiebeln abziehen und in Ringe schneiden
Peel the onions and slice them

7 Jetzt wird aufgeräumt!
You're going to clear up now!

8 Ruhe! Be quiet! Silence!
Vorsicht! Careful! Look out!

9 Achtung! Listen!/Attention!
Rauchen verboten! No smoking

Compound Tenses

The present and imperfect tenses in German are **simple** tenses, as described on pp.6 to 17.

All other tenses, called **compound tenses**, are formed for all types of verb by using the appropriate tense of an **auxiliary verb** plus a part of the main verb.

There are three auxiliary verbs:
>   **haben** for past tenses
>   **sein** also for past tenses
>   **werden** for future and conditional tenses

The **compound past tenses** in German are:

Perfect indicative	(→1)
Perfect subjunctive	(→2)
Pluperfect indicative	(→3)
Pluperfect subjunctive	(→4)

These are dealt with on pp.26 ff.

The **future** and **conditional tenses** in German are all compound tenses. They are:

Future indicative	(→5)
Future subjunctive	(→6)
Future perfect	(→7)
Conditional	(→8)
Conditional perfect	(→9)

These are dealt with on pp.28 ff.

	with **haben**	with **sein**
1	**er hat geholt** he (has) fetched	**er ist gereist** he (has) travelled
2	**er habe geholt** he (has) fetched	**er sei gereist** he (has) travelled
3	**er hatte geholt** he had fetched	**er war gereist** he had travelled
4	**er hätte geholt** he had fetched	**er wäre gereist** he had travelled
5	**er wird holen** he will fetch	**er wird reisen** he will travel
6	**er werde holen** he will fetch	**er werde reisen** he will travel
7	**er wird geholt haben** he will have fetched	**er wird gereist sein** he will have travelled
8	**er würde holen** he would fetch	**er würde reisen** he would travel
9	**er würde geholt haben** he would have fetched	**er würde gereist sein** he would have travelled

Compound Past Tenses: Formation

- Compound past tenses are normally formed by using the auxiliary verb **haben**, plus the past participle of the main verb (see below) (→**1**)

- Certain types of verb take **sein** instead of **haben**, and this is clearly indicated in the verb tables starting on p.86. They fall into three main types:
  1. intransitive verbs (those that take no direct object, often showing a change of state or place) (→**2**)
  2. certain verbs meaning "to happen" (→**3**)
  3. miscellaneous others, including:
     bleiben to remain, **gelingen** to succeed
     begegnen to meet, **sein** to be
     werden to become   (→**4**)

- In some cases the verb can be conjugated with either **haben** or **sein**, depending on whether it is used transitively (with a direct object) or intransitively (where no direct object is possible) (→**5**)

The Past Participle: Formation *(see also p.50)*

- **Weak** verbs add the prefix **ge-** and the suffix **-t** to the verb stem (→**6**)
  Verbs ending in **-ieren** or **-eien** omit the **ge-** (→**7**)

- **Strong** verbs add the prefix **ge-** and the suffix **-en** to the verb stem (→**8**). The vowel of the stem may be modified (see verb list, p.86) (→**9**)

- **Mixed** verbs add the prefix **ge-** and the "weak" suffix **-t** to the stem. The stem vowel is modified as for many strong verbs (→**10**)

Continued

1 Haben Sie gut geschlafen?
Did you sleep well?
Die Kinder hatten fleißig gearbeitet
The children had worked hard

2 Wir sind nach Bonn gefahren
We went to Bonn
Er ist schnell eingeschlafen
He quickly fell asleep

3 Was ist geschehen?
What happened?

4 Er ist zu Hause geblieben   **Er ist krank gewesen**
He stayed at home   He has been ill
Es ist uns nicht gelungen   **Sie ist krank geworden**
We did not succeed   She became ill
Er ist einem Freund begegnet
He met a friend

5 Er hat den Wagen nach Köln gefahren
He drove the car to Cologne
Er ist nach Köln gefahren
He went to Cologne

6 holen to fetch   **9 singen** to sing
   geholt fetched   **gesungen** sung

7 studieren to study   **10 senden** to send
   studiert studied   **gesandt** sent
   prophezeien to prophesy   **bringen** to bring
   prophezeit prophesied   **gebracht** brought

8 laufen to run
   gelaufen ran

For a full list of strong and mixed verbs see p.86

Compound Past Tenses: Formation (ctd.)

The formation of past participles for weak, strong and mixed verbs is described on p.24, and a comprehensive list of the principle parts of the most commonly used strong and mixed verbs is provided for reference on pp.86 to 97.

How to form the compound past tenses:

Perfect indicative	the present tense of **haben** or **sein** plus the past participle of the verb (→1)
Perfect subjunctive	(used in indirect or reported speech) the present subjunctive of **haben** or **sein** plus the past participle (→2)
Pluperfect indicative	imperfect indicative of **haben** or **sein** plus the past participle (→3)
Pluperfect subjunctive	(for indirect or reported speech) imperfect subjunctive of **haben** or **sein** plus the past participle (→4)

Note: The pluperfect subjunctive is a frequently used tense in German, since it can replace the much clumsier conditional perfect tense shown on p.28.

with **haben**	with **sein**

1 PERFECT INDICATIVE

ich habe geholt	ich bin gereist
du hast geholt	du bist gereist
er/sie/es hat geholt	er/sie/es ist gereist
wir haben geholt	wir sind gereist
ihr habt geholt	ihr seid gereist
sie/Sie haben geholt	sie/Sie sind gereist

2 PERFECT SUBJUNCTIVE

ich habe geholt	ich sei gereist
du habest geholt	du sei(e)st gereist
er/sie/es habe geholt	er/sie/es sei gereist
wir haben geholt	wir seien gereist
ihr habet geholt	ihr seiet gereist
sie/Sie haben geholt	sie/Sie seien gereist

3 PLUPERFECT INDICATIVE

ich hatte geholt	ich war gereist
du hattest geholt	du warst gereist
er/sie/es hatte geholt	er/sie/es war gereist
wir hatten geholt	wir waren gereist
ihr hattet geholt	ihr wart gereist
sie/Sie hatten geholt	sie/Sie waren gereist

4 PLUPERFECT SUBJUNCTIVE

ich hätte geholt	ich wäre gereist
du hättest geholt	du wär(e)st gereist
er/sie/es hätte geholt	er/sie/es wäre gereist
wir hätten geholt	wir wären gereist
ihr hättet geholt	ihr wär(e)t gereist
sie/Sie hätten geholt	sie/Sie wären gereist

Future and Conditional Tenses: Formation

● The **future** and **conditional** tenses are formed in the same way for all verbs, whether weak, strong or mixed.

● The auxiliary **werden** is used for all verbs together with the infinitive of the main verb

● The infinitive is usually placed at the end of the clause (see p.224).

How to form the future and conditional tenses:

Future indicative	present tense of **werden** plus the infinitive of the verb (→**1**)
Future subjunctive	present subjunctive of **werden** plus the infinitive (→**2**)
Future perfect	present indicative of **werden** plus the **perfect infinitive** (see below) (→**3**)
Conditional	imperfect subjunctive of **werden** plus the infinitive (→**4**)
Conditional perfect	imperfect subjunctive of **werden** plus the perfect infinitive (see below) (→**5**)
	Note: often replaced by the pluperfect subjunctive

● The **perfect infinitive** consists of the infinitive of **haben/sein** plus the past participle of the verb.

1 FUTURE INDICATIVE

ich werde holen	wir werden holen
du wirst holen	ihr werdet holen
er/sie/es wird holen	sie/Sie werden holen

2 FUTURE SUBJUNCTIVE

ich werde holen	wir werden holen
du werdest holen	ihr werdet holen
er/sie/es werde holen	sie/Sie werden holen

3 FUTURE PERFECT

ich werde geholt haben	wir werden geholt haben
du wirst geholt haben	ihr werdet geholt haben
er wird geholt haben	sie/Sie werden geholt haben

4 CONDITIONAL

ich würde holen	wir würden holen
du würdest holen	ihr würdet holen
er/sie/es würde holen	sie/Sie würden holen

5 CONDITIONAL PERFECT[1]

ich würde geholt haben	wir würden geholt haben
du würdest geholt haben	ihr würdet geholt haben
er würde geholt haben	sie/Sie würden geholt haben

1. *N.B. Often replaced by the pluperfect subjunctive (see p.26)*

Reflexive Verbs

A verb whose action is reflected back to its subject may be termed reflexive: *she* washes *herself*.

Reflexive verbs in German are recognized in the infinitive by the preceding reflexive pronoun **sich** (→1)

German has many reflexive verbs, a great number of which are not reflexive in English (→1)

● Reflexive verbs are composed of the verb and a reflexive pronoun (see p.170).
  This pronoun may be either the direct object (and therefore in the accusative case) or the indirect object (and therefore in the dative case) (→2)

● Many verbs in German which are not essentially reflexive may become reflexive by the addition of a reflexive pronoun (→3)
  When a verb with an indirect object is made reflexive (see p.170) the pronoun is usually dative (→4)

● A direct object reflexive pronoun changes to the dative if another direct object is present (→5)

● In a main clause the reflexive pronoun follows the verb (→6)
  After inversion (see p.226), or in a subordinate clause the reflexive pronoun must come after the subject if the subject is a personal pronoun (→7)
  It may precede or follow a noun subject (→8)

● Reflexive verbs are always conjugated with **haben** *except* where the pronoun is used to mean *each other*. Then the verb is normally conjugated with **sein**.

● The imperative forms are shown on p.19.

Continued

1 sich beeilen to hurry
   wir beeilen uns we are hurrying

2 sich (*accusative*) **erinnern**   **sich** (*dative*) **erlauben**
   to remember   to allow oneself
   ich erinnere mich   **ich erlaube mir**
   du erinnerst dich   **du erlaubst dir**
   er/sie/es erinnert sich   **er/sie/es erlaubt sich**
   wir erinnern uns   **wir erlauben uns**
   ihr erinnert euch   **ihr erlaubt euch**
   sie/Sie erinnern sich   **sie/Sie erlauben sich**

3 etwas melden to report something
      sich melden to report for/to volunteer for
      Ich habe mich gemeldet I volunteered

4 weh tun to hurt
      sich weh tun to get hurt
      Hast du dir weh getan? Have you hurt yourself?
   kaufen to buy
      Er kaufte ihr einen Mantel He bought her a coat
      Er kaufte sich (*dative*) **einen neuen Mantel**
      He bought himself a new coat

5 Ich wasche mich I am having a wash
   Ich wasche mir die Hände I am washing my hands

6 Er wird sich darüber freuen
   He'll be pleased about that

7 Darüber wird er sich freuen
   Ich frage mich, ob er sich darüber freuen wird
   I wonder if he'll be pleased about that

8 Langsam drehten sich die Kinder um
   OR
   Langsam drehten die Kinder sich um
   The children slowly turned around

Reflexive Verbs (ctd.)

Some examples of verbs which can be used with a reflexive pronoun in the accusative case:

sich anziehen to get dressed (→1)
sich aufregen to get excited (→2)
sich beeilen to hurry (→3)
sich beschäftigen mit[1] to be occupied with (→4)
sich bewerben um[1] to apply for (→5)
sich erinnern an[1] to remember (→6)
sich freuen auf[1] to look forward to (→7)
sich interessieren für[1] to be interested in (→8)
sich irren to be wrong (→9)
sich melden to report (for duty etc)
sich rasieren to shave
sich (hin)setzen to sit down (→10)
sich trauen[2] to trust oneself
sich umsehen to look around (→11)

Some examples of verbs which can be used with a reflexive pronoun in the dative case:

sich abgewöhnen to give up (something) (→12)
sich aneignen to appropriate
sich ansehen to have a look at
sich einbilden to imagine (wrongly) (→13)
sich erlauben to allow oneself (→14)
sich leisten to treat oneself (→15)
sich nähern to get close to
sich vornehmen to plan to do (→16)
sich vorstellen to imagine (→17)
sich wünschen to want (→18)

1. For verbs normally followed by a preposition, the reader is referred to p.76 ff.
2. **trauen** when non-reflexive takes the dative case.

1 Du sollst dich sofort anziehen
You are to get dressed immediately

2 Reg dich doch nicht so auf!
Calm down!

3 Wir müssen uns beeilen
We must hurry

4 Sie beschäftigen sich sehr mit den Kindern
They spend a lot of time with the children

5 Hast du dich um diese Stelle beworben?
Have you applied for this post?

6 Ich erinnere mich nicht daran
I can't remember it

7 Ich freue mich auf die Fahrt
I am looking forward to the journey

8 Interessierst du dich für Musik?
Are you interested in music?

9 Er hat sich geirrt
He was wrong

10 Bitte, setzt euch hin!
Please sit down

11 Die Kinder sahen sich erstaunt um
The children looked around in amazement

12 Eigentlich müßte man sich das Rauchen abgewöhnen
One really ought to give up smoking

13 Bilde dir doch nichts ein!
Don't kid yourself!

14 Eins könntest du dir doch erlauben
You could surely allow yourself one

15 Wenn ich mir nur einen Mercedes leisten könnte!
If only I could afford a Mercedes!

16 Du hast dir wieder zuviel vorgenommen!
You've taken on too much again!

17 So hatte ich es mir oft vorgestellt
I had often imagined it like this

18 Was wünscht ihr euch zu Weihnachten?
What do you want for Christmas?

The Passive

In active tenses, the subject of a verb carries out the action of the verb, but in passive tenses the subject of the verb has something done to it.
Compare the following:

> *Peter kicked the cat* (subject: *Peter*)
> *The cat was kicked by Peter* (subject: *the cat*)

● English uses the verb "to be" to form its passive tenses. German uses **werden** (→1)
  A sample verb is conjugated in the passive on pp.39 to 41.

● In English, the word "by" usually introduces the agent through which the action of a passive tense is performed. In German this agent is introduced by:
  von for the performer of the action
  durch for an inanimate cause (→2)

● The passive can be used to add impersonality or distance to an event (→3)
  It may also be used where the identity of the cause of the deed is unknown or not important (→4)

● In general however the passive is used less in German than in English. The following are common replacements for the passive:

  1. an active tense with the impersonal pronoun **man** as subject (meaning *they/one*). This resembles the use of *on* in French, and **man** is not always translated as *one* or *they* (→5)

  2. **sich lassen** plus a verb in the infinitive (→6)

Continued

1 Das Auto wurde gekauft
The car was bought

2 Das ist von seinem Onkel geschickt worden
It was sent by his uncle
Das Kind wurde von einem Hund gebissen
The child was bitten by a dog
Seine Bewerbung ist von der Firma abgelehnt worden
(*the firm is viewed as a human agent*)
His application was turned down by the firm

Die Tür wurde durch den Wind geöffnet
The door was opened by the wind
Das Getreide wurde durch den Sturm niedergeschlagen
The crop was flattened by the storm

3 Die Praxis ist von Dr. Lehmann übernommen worden
The practice has been taken over by Dr Lehmann
Anfang 1767 wurde noch ein Anschlag auf sein Leben gemacht
Another attempt was made on his life early in 1767

4 In letzter Zeit sind neue Gesetze eingeführt worden
New laws have recently been introduced

5 Man hatte es schon verkauft
It had already been sold
Man wird es verkauft haben
It will have been sold

6 Das läßt sich schnell herausfinden
We'll/You'll/One will be able to find that out quickly

The Passive (ctd.)

● In English the indirect object of an active tense can become the subject of a passive statement. e.g.

> Peter gave *him* a car (*him* = to him)
> *He* was given a car by Peter

This is not possible in German, where the indirect object (*him*) must remain in the dative case (see p. 110). There are two ways of handling this in German:
1. with the direct object (*car*) as the subject of a passive verb (→**1**)
2. by means of an impersonal passive construction, with or without the impersonal subject **es** (→**1**)

These constructions would however normally be avoided in favour of an active tense, when the agent of the action is known (→**2**)

● Verbs which are normally followed by the dative case in German and so have only an indirect object (see p.80) should therefore be especially noted, as they can only adopt the impersonal or **man**-forms of the passive (→**3**)

● Some passive tenses are avoided in German, as they are inelegant (and difficult to use!). For instance, the future perfect passives should be replaced by an active tense or a **man**-construction (→**4**)

The conditional perfect passives are also rarely used, past conditional being shown by the pluperfect subjunctives, either passive or active (→**5**)

● English passive constructions such as
> *he was heard whistling/they were thought to be dying*

are not possible in German (→**6**)

Continued

1 **Ein Auto wurde ihm von Peter gegeben**
   OR :
   Es wurde ihm von Peter ein Auto gegeben
   OR :
   Ihm wurde von Peter ein Auto gegeben
   He was given a car by Peter

2 **Peter gab ihm ein Auto**
   Peter gave him a car

3 **helfen** (+ *dative*)   to help :

Sie half mir	**Mir wurde von ihr geholfen**
She helped me →	OR
	Es wurde mir von ihr geholfen
	I was helped by her

4 **Er meint, es werde schon gesehen worden sein**
   He thinks that it will already have been seen

   BETTER : **Er meint, man werde es schon gesehen haben**

5 **Es würde geholt worden sein / Man würde es geholt haben**
   It would have been fetched

   BETTER : **Es wäre geholt worden / Man hätte es geholt**

6 **Man hörte ihn singen**
   He was heard singing
   Man sah es ankommen
   It was seen arriving
   Man glaubte, er sei betrunken
   He was thought to be drunk

Passive Tenses: Conjugation

Simple Tenses

Present passive indicative
e.g. *it is seen*

present indicative of **werden** + past participle of the verb (→**1**)

Present passive subjunctive

present subjunctive of **werden** + past participle of the verb (→**2**)

Imperfect passive indicative
e.g. *it was seen*

imperfect indicative of **werden** + past participle of the verb (→**3**)

Imperfect passive subjunctive

imperfect subjunctive of **werden** + past participle of the verb (→**4**)

Compound Tenses

Perfect passive indicative
e.g. *it has been seen*

present indicative of **sein** + past participle of the verb + **worden** (→**5**)

Perfect passive subjunctive

present subjunctive of **sein** + past participle of the verb + **worden** (→**6**)

Pluperfect passive indicative
e.g. *it had been seen*

imperfect indicative of **sein** + past participle + **worden** (→**7**)

Continued

1 PRESENT PASSIVE INDICATIVE

ich werde gesehen	**wir werden gesehen**
du wirst gesehen	**ihr werdet gesehen**
er/sie/es wird gesehen	**sie/Sie werden gesehen**

OR: **man sieht mich/man sieht dich** *etc*

2 PRESENT PASSIVE SUBJUNCTIVE

ich werde gesehen	**wir werden gesehen**
du werdest gesehen	**ihr werdet gesehen**
er/sie/es werde gesehen	**sie/Sie werden gesehen**

OR: **man sehe mich/man sehe dich** *etc*

3 IMPERFECT PASSIVE INDICATIVE
ich wurde gesehen/wir wurden gesehen *etc*

OR: **man sah mich/ man sah uns** *etc*

4 IMPERFECT PASSIVE SUBJUNCTIVE
ich würde gesehen/wir würden gesehen *etc*

OR: **man sähe mich/man sähe uns** *etc*

5 PERFECT PASSIVE INDICATIVE
ich bin gesehen worden/wir sind gesehen worden *etc*

OR: **man hat mich/uns gesehen** *etc*

6 PERFECT PASSIVE SUBJUNCTIVE
ich sei gesehen worden/wir seien gesehen worden *etc*

OR: **man habe mich/uns gesehen** *etc*

7 PLUPERFECT PASSIVE INDICATIVE
ich war gesehen worden/wir waren gesehen worden *etc*

OR: **man hatte mich/uns gesehen** *etc*

Passive Tenses: Conjugation (ctd.)

Pluperfect passive subjunctive	imperfect subjunctive of **sein** + past participle of the verb + **worden** (→1)
Present passive infinitive e.g. *it will be seen*	infinitive of **werden** + past participle of the verb (→2)
Future passive indicative e.g. *it will be seen*	present indicative of **werden** + present passive infinitive of the verb (→3)
Future passive subjunctive	present subjunctive of **werden** + present passive infinitive (→4)
Perfect passive infinitive e.g. *to have been seen*	past participle of the verb + **worden sein** (→5)
Future perfect passive e.g. *it will have been seen*	present indicative of **werden** + perfect passive infinitive of the verb (→6)
Conditional passive e.g. *it would be seen*	imperfect subjunctive of of **werden** + present passive infinitive of the verb (→7)
Conditional perfect passive e.g. *it would have been seen*	imperfect subjunctive of **werden** + perfect passive infinitive of the verb (→8)

1 PLUPERFECT PASSIVE SUBJUNCTIVE
ich wäre gesehen worden/wir wären gesehen worden *etc*

OR: **man hätte mich/uns gesehen** *etc*

2 PRESENT PASSIVE INFINITIVE
gesehen werden

3 FUTURE PASSIVE INDICATIVE
ich werde gesehen werden/wir werden gesehen werden *etc*

OR: **man wird mich/uns sehen** *etc*

4 FUTURE PASSIVE SUBJUNCTIVE
ich werde gesehen werden/wir werden gesehen werden *etc*

OR: **man werde mich/uns sehen** *etc*

5 PERFECT PASSIVE INFINITIVE
gesehen worden sein

6 FUTURE PERFECT PASSIVE
ich werde/wir werden gesehen worden sein *etc*

OR: **man wird mich/uns gesehen haben** *etc*

7 CONDITIONAL PASSIVE
ich würde gesehen werden/wir würden gesehen werden

OR: **man würde mich/uns sehen** *etc*

8 CONDITIONAL PERFECT PASSIVE
ich würde/wir würden gesehen worden sein

OR: **man würde mich/uns gesehen haben** *etc*
OR: pluperfect subjunctive: **man hätte mich/uns gesehen** *etc*

Impersonal Verbs

These verbs are used only in the third person singular, usually with the subject **es** meaning *it* (→1)

- Intransitive verbs (verbs with no direct object) are often made impersonal in the passive to describe activity of a general nature (→2)
  When the verb and subject are inverted (see p.226), the **es** is omitted (→3)
  Impersonal verbs in the passive can also be used as an imperative form (see p.20) (→4)

- In certain expressions in the active, the impersonal pronoun **es** can be omitted. In this case, a personal pronoun object begins the clause (→5)
  In the following lists * indicates that **es** may be omitted in this way:

Some common impersonal verbs and expressions

es donnert *it's thundering*
es fällt mir ein, daß/zu★ *it occurs to me that/to* (→6)
es fragt sich, ob *one wonders whether* (→7)
es freut mich, daß/zu *I am glad that/to* (→8)
es friert *it is freezing* (→9)
es gefällt mir *I like it* (→10)
es geht mir gut/schlecht *I'm fine/not too good*
es geht nicht *it's not possible*
es geht um *it's about*
es gelingt mir, (zu) *I succeed (in)* (→11)
es geschieht *it happens* (→12)
es gießt *it's pouring*
es handelt sich um *it's a question of*
Continued

1 Es regnet It's raining

2 Es wurde viel gegessen und getrunken
There was a lot of eating and drinking

3 Auf der Hochzeit wurde viel gegessen und getrunken
There was a lot of eating and drinking at the wedding

4 Jetzt wird gearbeitet! Now you're going to work

5 Mir ist warm I'm warm

**6 Nachher fiel (es) mir ein, daß der Mann ziemlich komisch
angezogen war**
Afterwards it occurred to me that the man was rather oddly
dressed

7 Es fragt sich, ob es sich lohnt, das zu machen
One wonders if that's worth doing

8 Es freut mich sehr, daß du gekommen bist
I'm so pleased that you have come

9 Heute nacht hat es gefroren
It was below freezing last night

10 Ihm hat es gar nicht gefallen
He didn't like it at all

11 Es war ihnen gelungen, die letzten Karten zu kriegen
They had succeeded in getting the last tickets

12 Und so geschah es, daß ...
And so it came about that ...

Impersonal Verbs and Expressions (ctd.)

es hängt davon ab *it depends*
es hat keinen Zweck (zu) *there's no point (in)* (→1)
es interessiert mich, daß/zu* *I am interested that/to*
es ist mir egal (ob)* *it's all the same to me (if)* (→2)
es ist möglich (, daß) *it's possible (that)* (→3)
es ist nötig *it's necessary* (→4)
es ist mir, als ob* *I feel as if*
es ist mir gut/schlecht *etc* zumute* *I feel good /bad etc* (→5)
es ist schade (,daß) *it's a pity (that)*
es ist (mir) wichtig* *it's important (to me)*
es ist mir warm/kalt* *I'm hot/cold*
es ist warm/kalt *it's (the weather is) warm/cold*
es ist zu hoffen/bedauern *etc* *it is to be hoped etc*
es klingelt *someone is ringing the bell* (→6)
es klopft *someone's knocking*
es kommt darauf an (, ob) *it all depends (whether)*
es kommt mir vor (, als ob) *it seems to me (as if)*
es läutet *the bell is ringing* (→7)
es liegt an *it is because of* (→8)
es lohnt sich (nicht) *it's (not) worth it* (→9)
es macht nichts *it doesn't matter*
es macht nichts aus *it makes no difference* (→10)
es macht mir (keinen) Spaß (, zu) *it's (no) fun (to)* (→11)
es passiert *it happens* (→12)
es regnet *it's raining* (→13)
es scheint mir, daß/als ob* *it seems to me that/as if*
es schneit *it's snowing*
es stellt sich heraus, daß *it turns out that*
es stimmt (nicht), daß *it's (not) true, that*
es tut mir leid (, daß) *I'm sorry (that)*
wie geht es (dir)? *how are you?* (→14)
mir wird schlecht* *I feel sick*

1 Es hat keinen Zweck, weiter darüber zu diskutieren
There's no point in discussing this any further

2 Es ist mir egal, ob du kommst oder nicht
I don't care if you come or not

3 Es ist doch möglich, daß der Zug Verspätung hat
It's always possible the train has been delayed

4 Es wird nicht nötig sein, uns darüber zu informieren
It won't be necessary to inform us of it

5 Mir ist heute seltsam zumute I feel strange today

6 Es hat gerade geklingelt
The bell just went/The phone just rang

7 Es hat schon geläutet The bell has gone

8 Woran liegt es? Why is that?

9 Ich weiß nicht, ob es sich lohnt oder nicht
I don't know if it's worth it or not

10 Mir macht es nichts aus It makes no difference to me
Macht es Ihnen etwas aus, wenn ... Would you mind if...

11 Hauptsache, es macht Spaß
The main thing is to enjoy yourself

12 Ihm ist bestimmt etwas passiert
Something must have happened to him

13 Es hat den ganzen Tag geregnet It rained the whole day

14 Wie geht's denn? — Danke, es geht
How are things? — Fine thank you

The Infinitive

Forms

There are four forms of the infinitive (→**1**). These forms are used in forming certain compound tenses (see p.28). The present active infinitive is the most widely used and is the form found in dictionaries.

Uses

● Preceded by **zu** (*to*)

1. as in English, after other verbs ("I tried *to come*") (→**2**)
2. as in English, after adjectives ("it was easy *to see*") (→**3**)
3. where the English equivalent is not always an infinitive:
   — after nouns, where English may use an "-ing" form (→**4**)
   — after **sein**, where the English equivalent may be a passive tense (→**5**)

● Without **zu**, the infinitive is used after the following:

   modal verbs (→**6**)
   lassen (→**7**)
   heißen (→**8**)
   bleiben (→**9**)
   gehen (→**10**)
   verbs of perception (→**11**)
   NOTE: verbs of perception can also be followed by a subordinate clause beginning with **wie** or **daß**, especially if the sentence is long or involved (→**12**)

Continued

1 INFINITIVES:

PRESENT ACTIVE
holen
to fetch

PRESENT PASSIVE
geholt werden
to be fetched

PERFECT ACTIVE
geholt haben
to have fetched

PERFECT PASSIVE
geholt worden sein
to have been fetched

2 Ich versuchte, zu kommen I tried to come

3 Es war leicht, zu sehen It was easy to see

4 Ich habe nur wenig Gelegenheit, Musik zu hören
I have little opportunity of listening to music

5 Er ist zu bedauern He is to be pitied

6 Er kann schwimmen He can swim

7 Sie ließen uns warten They kept us waiting

8 Er hieß ihn kommen He bade him come

9 Er blieb sitzen He remained seated

10 Sie ging einkaufen She went shopping

11 Ich sah ihn kommen I saw him coming
Er hörte sie singen He heard her singing

12 Er sah, wie sie langsam auf und ab schlenderte
He watched her strolling slowly up and down

The Infinitive (ctd.)

Used as an imperative
● The infinitive can be used as an imperative (see p.20) (→**1**)

Used as a noun
● The infinitive can be made into a noun by giving it a capital letter. Its gender is always neuter (→**2**)

Used with modal verbs (see p.52)
● An infinitive used with a modal verb is always placed at the end of a clause (see p.56) (→**3**)

● If the modal verb is in a compound tense, its auxiliary will follow the subject in a main clause in the normal way, and the modal participle comes after the infinitive. BUT in a subordinate clause, the auxiliary immediately precedes the infinitive and the modal participle, instead of coming at the end (→**4**)

● An infinitive expressing change of place may be omitted entirely after a modal verb (see p.56) (→**5**)

Used in infinitive phrases
Infinitive phrases can be formed with:

zu	ohne ... zu
um ... zu	anstatt ... zu (→**6**)

● The infinitive comes at the end of its phrase (→**7**)

● In separable verbs, **zu** is inserted *between* the verb and its prefix in the present infinitive (→**8**)

● A reflexive pronoun comes first, immediately following an introductory word if there is one (→**9**)

1   **Einsteigen und Türen schließen!**
All aboard! Close the doors!

2   **rauchen** to smoke:
Er hat das Rauchen aufgegeben
He's given up smoking

3   **Wir müssen morgen einkaufen gehen**
We have to go shopping tomorrow

4   **Sie haben gestern aufräumen müssen**
They had to tidy up yesterday
BUT
**Da sie gestern haben aufräumen müssen, durften sie nicht
kommen**
They couldn't come as they had to tidy up yesterday

5   **Er will jetzt nach Hause** He wants to go home now

6   **es zu tun** to do it
es getan zu haben to have done it
um es zu tun in order to do it
um es getan zu haben in order to have done it
ohne es zu tun without doing it
ohne es getan zu haben without having done it
anstatt es zu tun instead of doing it
anstatt es getan zu haben instead of having done it

7   **Ohne ein Wort zu sagen, verließ er das Haus**
He left the house without saying a word
Er ging nach Hause, ohne mit ihr gesprochen zu haben
He went home without having spoken to her

8   **aufgeben** to give up:
um es aufzugeben in order to give it up

9   **Sie gingen weg, ohne sich zu verabschieden**
They left without saying goodbye

The Present Participle

- The present participle for all verbs is formed by adding **-d** to the infinitive form (→1)

- The present participle may be used as an adjective. As with all adjectives, it is declined if used attributively (see p.140) (→2)

- The present participle may also be used as an adjectival noun (see p.148) (→3)

The Past Participle

- For weak verbs, the past participle is formed by prefixing **ge-** and adding **-t** to the verb stem (→4)

- For strong verbs, the past participle is formed by adding the prefix **ge-** and the ending **-en** to the verb stem (→5) The vowel is often modified too (→6) (See list of strong and mixed verbs beginning on p.86)

- Mixed verbs form their past participle by adding the **ge-** and **-t** of weak verbs, but they change their vowel as for strong verbs. (See list, p.86) (→7)

- The past participles of *separable* verbs are formed according to the above rules and are joined on to the separable prefix (→8)

- For *inseparable* verbs, past participles are formed without the **ge-** prefix (→9)

- Many past participles can also be used as adjectives and adjectival nouns (→10)

1 lachen to laugh
lachend laughing

singen to sing
singend singing

2 ein lachendes Kind a laughing child
mit klopfendem Herzen with beating heart

3 der Vorsitzende/ein Vorsitzender the/a chairman

4 machen to do/make
gemacht done/made

5 sehen to see
gesehen seen

6 singen to sing
gesungen sung

7 wissen to know
gewußt known

8 aufstehen to get up
aufgestanden got up

nachmachen to copy/imitate
nachgemacht imitated

9 bestellen to order
bestellt ordered

entscheiden to decide
entschieden decided

10 seine verlorene Brille his lost spectacles
Wir aßen Gebratenes We ate fried food

Modal Auxiliary Verbs

Modal verbs, sometimes called modal auxiliaries, are used to
modify other verbs (to show e.g. possibility, ability,
willingness, permission, necessity) much as in English:

> he *can* swim; *may* I come?; we *shouldn't* go

● In German the modal auxiliary verbs are: **dürfen,
können, mögen, müssen, sollen** and **wollen**.

● Modal verbs have some important differences in their uses
and in their conjugation from other verbs, and these are
clearly shown on pp.86 to 97.

● Modal verbs have the following meanings :

dürfen   to be *allowed to/may* (→**1**)
used negatively: *must not/may not* (→**2**)
to show probability (→**3**)
also used in some polite expressions (→**4**)

können   to be *able to, can* (→**5**)
in its subjunctive forms:
would be able to/could (→**6**)
as an informal alternative to **dürfen** with the
meaning: *allowed to/can* (→**7**)
to show possibility (→**8**)

mögen   *to like/to like to* (→**9**)
most common in its imperfect subjunctive
form which expresses polite inquiry or request:
should like to/would like to (→**10**)
to show possibility or probability (→**11**)

Continued

1 Darfst du mit ins Kino kommen?
Are you allowed to (can you) come with us to the cinema?
Darf ich bitte mitkommen?
May I come with you please?
Ich dürfte schon, aber ich will nicht
I could (would be allowed to), but I don't want to

2 Hier darf man nicht rauchen
Smoking is prohibited here

3 Das dürfte wohl das Beste sein
That's probably the best thing

4 Was darf es sein?
Can I help you?/What would you like?

5 Wir konnten es nicht schaffen
We couldn't (weren't able to) do it.

6 Er könnte noch früher kommen
He could (would be able to) come even earlier
Er meinte, er könne noch früher kommen
He thought he could come earlier
Wir könnten vielleicht morgen hinfahren?
Perhaps we could go there tomorrow?

7 Kann ich (darf ich) ein Eis haben?
Can I (may I) have an ice-cream?

8 Wer könnte es gewesen sein?
Who could it have been?
Das kann sein
That may be so
BUT: **Das kann nicht sein** That cannot be so

9 Magst du Butter?
Do you like butter?

10 Wir möchten bitte etwas trinken
We should like something to drink
Möchtest du sie besuchen?
Would you like to visit her?

11 Das Konzert mochte vier Stunden gedauert haben
The concert must have lasted four hours

Modal Auxiliary Verbs (ctd.)

müssen   *to have to/must/need to* (→**1**)
              certain idiomatic uses (→**2**)

              NOTE: for *must have ...*, use the relevant tense
              of **müssen** + past participle of main verb +
              the auxiliary **haben** or **sein** (→**3**)
              for *don't have to/need not*, a negative form of
              brauchen (*to need*) may be used instead of
              müssen (→**4**)

sollen   *ought to/should* (→**5**)
              to be (supposed) to where the demand is not self-
              imposed (→**6**)
              to be said to be (→**7**)
              as a command, either direct or indirect (→**8**)

wollen   *to want/want to* (→**9**)
              used as a less formal version of **mögen** to
              mean: *want/wish* (→**10**)
              to be willing to (→**11**)
              to show previous intention (→**12**)
              to claim or pretend (→**13**)

Continued

1 Er hatte jeden Tag um sechs aufstehen müssen
He had to get up at six o'clock every day
Man mußte lachen
One had to laugh/couldn't help laughing

2 Muß das sein? Is that really necessary?
Ein Millionär müßte man sein!
Oh to be a millionaire!
Den Film muß man gesehen haben
That film is worth seeing

3 Es muß geregnet haben It must have been raining
Er meinte, es müsse am vorigen Abend passiert sein
He thought it must have happened the previous evening

4 Das brauchtest du nicht zu sagen
You didn't have to say that

5 Man sollte immer die Wahrheit sagen
One should always tell the truth
Er wußte nicht, was er tun sollte
He didn't know what to do (*what he should do*)

6 Ich soll dir helfen
I am to help you (*I have been told to help you*)
Du sollst sofort deine Frau anrufen
You are to 'phone your wife at once (*She has left a message asking you to ring*)

7 Er soll sehr reich sein
I've heard he's very rich/He is said to be very rich

8 Es soll niemand sagen, daß die Schotten geizig sind!
Let no-one say the Scots are mean!
Sie sagte mir, ich solle damit aufhören
She told me to stop it

9 Das Kind will LKW-Fahrer werden
The child wants to become a lorry driver

10 Willst du eins? Do you want one?
Willst du (möchtest du) etwas trinken?
Do you want (would you like) something to drink?

11 Er wollte nichts sagen He refused to say anything

12 Ich wollte gerade anrufen I was just about to 'phone

13 Keiner will es gewesen sein No-one admits to doing it

Modal Auxiliary Verbs (ctd.)

Conjugation and Use

- Modal verbs have unusual present tenses (→1)
  Their principal parts are given on pp.86 to 97.

- Each modal verb has two past participles.
  The first, which is the more common, is the same as the infinitive form and is used where the modal is modifying a verb (→2)
  The second resembles a normal weak past participle and is used only where no verb is being modified (see the verb list, p.86) (→3)

- The verb modified by the modal is placed in its infinitive form at the end of a clause (→4)

- Where the modal is used in a compound tense, its past participle in the form of the infinitive is also placed at the end of a clause, immediately after the modified verb (→5)

- If the modal verb is modifying a verb, and if the modal is used in a compound tense in a subordinate clause, then the normal word order for subordinate clauses (see p.228) does not apply. The auxiliary used to form the compound tense of the modal is not placed right at the end of the subordinate clause, but instead comes before both infinitives (→6)
  Such constructions are usually avoided in German, by using a simple tense in place of a compound. (For notes on the use of tenses in German, see p.58ff) (→7)

- A modified verb which expresses motion may be omitted entirely if an adverb or adverbial phrase is present to indicate the movement or destination (→8)

1

dürfen	**können**
ich/er/sie/es darf	ich/er/sie/es kann
du darfst	du kannst
wir/sie/Sie dürfen	wir/sie/Sie können
ihr dürft	ihr könnt

mögen	**müssen**
ich/er/sie/es mag	ich/er/sie/es muß
du magst	du mußt
wir/sie/Sie mögen	wir/sie/Sie müssen
ihr mögt	ihr müßt

sollen	**wollen**
ich/er/sie/es soll	ich/er/sie/es will
du sollst	du willst
wir/sie/Sie sollen	wir/sie/Sie wollen
ihr sollt	ihr wollt

2 **wollen**: Past participle **wollen**
    er hat kommen wollen he wanted to come

3 **wollen**: Past participle **gewollt**
    Hast du es gewollt? Did you want it?

4 **Er kann gut schwimmen** He can swim well

5 **Wir haben das Haus nicht kaufen wollen**
    We didn't want to buy the house
    Sie wird dich bald sehen wollen
    She will want to see you soon

6 *Compare*:
    Obwohl wir das Haus gekauft haben, ...
    Although we bought the house
    Obwohl wir das Haus haben kaufen wollen, ...
    Although we wanted to buy the house

7 **Obwohl wir das Haus kaufen wollten ...**
    Although we wanted to buy the house

8 **Ich muß nach Hause** I must go home
    Die Kinder sollen jetzt ins Bett
    The children have to go to bed now

Use of Tenses

Continuous Forms
- Unlike English, the German verb does not distinguish between its simple and continuous forms (→1)
- To emphasize continuity, the following may be used:
  simple tense plus an adverb or adverbial phrase (→2)
  am or **beim** plus an infinitive used as a noun (→3)
  eben/gerade dabei sein zu plus an infinitive (→4)

The Present
- The present tense is used in German with **seit** or **seitdem** where English uses a past tense to show an action which began in the past and still continues (→5)
  If the action is finished, or does not continue, a past tense is used (→6)
- The present is commonly used with future meaning (→7)

The Future
- The present is often used as a future tense (→7)
- The future tense is used however to:
  emphasise the future (→8)
  express doubt or supposition about the future (→9)
  express future intention (→10)

The Future Perfect
- Used as in English to mean *shall/will have done* (→11)
- It is used in German to express a supposition (→12)
- In conversation it is replaced by the perfect (→13)

The Conditional
- May be used in place of the imperfect subjunctive to express improbable condition (see p.62) (→14)
- Is used in indirect statements or questions to replace the future subjunctive in conversation or where the subjunctive form is not distinctive (→15)

Continued

1 ich tue I do (*simple form*) OR I am doing (*continuous*)
  er rauchte he smoked OR he was smoking
  sie hat gelesen she has read OR she has been reading
  es ist geschickt worden it is sent OR it is being sent

2 Er kochte gerade das Abendessen
  He was cooking the supper
  Nun spricht sie mit ihm Now she's talking to him

3 Ich bin am Bügeln I am ironing

4 Wir waren eben dabei, einige Briefe zu schreiben
  We were just writing a few letters

5 Ich wohne seit zehn Jahren hier
  I have been living here for ten years
  Seit ich hier wohne, fühle ich mich wohl
  I've been feeling at home since I've lived here

6 Seit er krank ist, hat er uns nicht besucht
  He hasn't visited us since he's been ill
  Seit seiner Verlobung habe ich ihn nicht gesehen
  I haven't seen him since his engagement

7 Ich komme morgen vorbei I'll come round tomorrow
  Wir fahren nächstes Jahr nach Griechenland
  We're going to Greece next year

8 Das werde ich erst nächstes Jahr machen können
  I won't be able to do that until next year

9 Wenn er zurückkommt, wird er mir bestimmt helfen
  He's sure to help me when he returns

10 Ich werde ihm helfen I'm going to help him

11 Bis Sonntag wird er es gelesen haben
  He will have read it by Sunday

12 Es wird Herr Schmidt gewesen sein
  That must have been Herr Schmidt

13 Bis du zurückkommst, haben wir alles aufgeräumt
  We'll have tidied up by the time you get back

14 Wenn ich eins hätte, würde ich es dir geben
  If I had one I would give it to you
  Wenn er jetzt bloß kommen würde!
  If only he would get here!

15 Er fragte, ob wir fahren würden
  He asked if we were going to go

Use of Tenses (ctd.)

The Conditional Perfect
- May be used in place of the pluperfect subjunctive in a sentence containing a **wenn**-clause (→1)
- But the pluperfect subjunctive is preferred (→2)

The Imperfect
- Is used in German with **seit** or **seitdem** where the pluperfect is used in English to show an action which began in the remote past and continued to a point in the more recent past (→3)

  For discontinued actions the pluperfect is used (→4)
- Used to describe past actions which have no link with the present as far as the speaker is concerned (→5)

  for narrative purposes (→6)

  for repeated, habitual or prolonged past action (→7)

See also the note on the **Perfect** (below).

The Perfect
- Is used to translate the English perfect tense *I have spoken, he has been reading* (→8)
- Describes past actions or events which still have a link with the present or the speaker (→9)
- Is used in conversation and similar communication (→10)

NOTE: In practice however the perfect and imperfect are often interchangeable in German usage and in spoken German a mixture of both is common.

The Pluperfect
- Is used to translate *had done/had been doing*, except in conjunction with **seit/seitdem** (see Imperfect) (→11)

The Subjunctive
For uses of the subjunctive tenses, see pp.62 to 67.

1 Wenn du es gesehen hättest, würdest du's geglaubt haben
You would have believed it if you'd seen it

2 Hättest du es gesehen, so hättest du es geglaubt
If you had seen it, you'd have believed it
Wenn ich das nur nicht gemacht hätte!
If only I hadn't done it!
Wäre ich nur da gewesen! If I'd only been there

3 Sie war seit ihrer Heirat als Krankenschwester beschäftigt
She had been working as a nurse since her marriage

4 Ihren Sohn hatten sie seit zehn Jahren nicht gesehen
They hadn't seen their son for ten years

5 Er kam zu spät, um teilnehmen zu können
He arrived too late to take part

6 Das Mädchen stand auf, wusch sich das Gesicht, und verließ das Haus
The girl got up, washed her face and went out

7 Wir machten jeden Tag einen kleinen Spaziergang
We went (used to go) for a little walk every day

8 Ich habe ihn heute nicht gesehen
I haven't seen him today

9 Ich habe ihr nichts davon erzählt
I didn't tell her anything about it
Gestern sind wir in die Stadt gefahren, und haben uns ein Paar Sachen gekauft
Yesterday we went into town and bought ourselves a few things

10 Hast du den Krimi gestern abend im Fernsehen gesehen?
Did you see the thriller on television last night?

11 Sie waren schon weggefahren
They had already left
Diese Bücher hatten sie schon gelesen
They had already read these books

The Subjunctive: when to use it

The subjunctive form in English has almost died out, leaving only a few examples such as:

if I *were* rich/if only he *were* to come/so *be* it

German however makes much wider use of subjunctive forms, especially in formal, educated or literary contexts. Although there is a growing tendency to use indicatives in spoken German, subjunctives are still very common.

● The indicative tenses in German display fact or certainty. The subjunctives show unreality, uncertainty, speculation about a situation or any doubt in the speaker's mind (→**1**) Subjunctives are also used in indirect speech, as shown on pp.66 and 67.

● For how to form all tenses of the subjunctive, the reader is referred to the relevant sections on Simple Tenses (pp.6 to 17) and Compound Tenses (pp.22 to 29). See also the Subjunctive in Reported Speech p.66.

● The **imperfect subjunctive** is very common. It is important to note that the imperfect subjunctive form does not always represent actions performed in the past (→**2**)

Uses of the Subjunctive in German

● To show improbable condition (e.g. if he *came*, he would ...)
The *if*-clause (**wenn** in German) has a verb in the imperfect subjunctive and the main clause can have either an imperfect subjunctive or a conditional (→**3**)

Continued

1 INDICATIVE
Das stimmt
That's true
Es ist eine Unverschämtheit
It's a scandal

SUBJUNCTIVE
Es könnte doch wahr sein
It could well be true
Sie meint, es sei eine Unverschämtheit
She thinks it's a scandal (*speaker not necessarily in agreement with her*)

2 *imperfect subjunctive expressing the future*
Wenn ich morgen nur da sein könnte!
If only I could be there tomorrow!

expressing the present/immediate future
Wenn er jetzt nur käme!
If only he would come now!

speaker's opinion, referring to present or future
Sie wäre die Beste
She's the best

3 **Wenn du kämest, wäre ich froh**
OR
Wenn du kämest, würde ich froh sein
I should be happy if you came

Wenn es mir nicht gefiele, würde ich es nicht bezahlen
OR
Wenn es mir nicht gefiele, bezahlte ich es nicht
If I wasn't happy with it, I wouldn't pay for it
(*The second form is less likely, as the imperfect subjunctive and imperfect indicative forms of* **bezahlen** *are identical*)

The Subjunctive: when to use it (ctd.)

- The imperfect of **sollen** or **wollen**, or a conditional tense might be used in the **wenn**-clause to replace an uncommon imperfect subjunctive, or a subjunctive which is not distinct from the same tense of the indicative (→1)

- To show unfulfilled condition (if he *had come*, he would have...)
  The **wenn**-clause requires a pluperfect subjunctive, the main clause a pluperfect subjunctive or conditional perfect (→2)
  NOTE: The indicative is used to express a *probable* condition, as in English (→3)
  wenn can be omitted from conditional clauses. The verb must then follow the subject and **dann** or **so** usually begins the main clause (→4)

- With **selbst wenn** (*even if/even though*) (→5)

- With **wenn ... nur** (*if only ...*) (→6)

- To speculate or make assumptions (→7)

- After **als** (*as if/as though*) (→8)

- Where there is uncertainty or doubt (→9)

- To make a polite enquiry (→10)

- To indicate theoretical possibility or unreality (→11)

- As an alternative to the conditional perfect (→12)

1 Wenn er mich so sehen würde, würde er mich für verrückt halten!

OR

Wenn er mich so sehen sollte, hielte er mich für verrückt!

OR

Wenn er mich so sehen sollte, würde er mich für verrückt halten!

If he saw me like this, he would think I was mad!

(**Wenn er mich so sähe** *would sound rather stilted*)

2 Wenn du pünktlich gekommen wärest, hättest du ihn gesehen

OR

Wenn du pünktlich gekommen wärest, würdest du ihn gesehen haben

If you had been on time, you would have seen him

3 Wenn ich ihn sehe, gebe ich es ihm

If I see him I'll give him it

4 Hättest du mich nicht gesehen, so wäre ich schon weg

If you hadn't seen me, I would have been gone by now

5 Selbst wenn er etwas wüßte, würde er nichts sagen

Even if he knew about it, he wouldn't say anything

6 Wenn wir nur reich wären! If only we were rich!

7 Und wenn er recht hätte? What if he were right?

Eine Frau, die das sagen würde (*or* **die das sagte), müßte Feministin sein!**

Any woman who would say that must be a feminist!

8 Er sah aus, als sei er krank

He looked as if he were ill

9 Er wußte nicht, wie es ihr jetzt ginge

He didn't know how she was

10 Gäbe es sonst was? Will there be anything else?

11 Er dachte, wie er in dem Anzug gut aussähe

He thought how good he would look in the suit

12 Ich hätte ihn gesehen = Ich würde ihn gesehen haben

I would have seen him

The Subjunctive in Indirect Speech

What a person asks or thinks can be reported in one of two ways, either **directly**:

Tom said, "*I have been on holiday*"

OR **indirectly**:

Tom said (that) *he had been on holiday*

- In English, indirect, or reported, speech can be indicated by a change in tense of what has been reported:

    He said, "*I know your sister*"

    He said (that) *he knew my sister*

    In German the change is not in tense, but from indicative to subjunctive (→1)

- There are two ways of introducing indirect speech in German, similar to the parallel English constructions:
    1. The clause which reports what is said may be introduced by **daß** (*that*). The finite verb or auxiliary comes at the end of the clause (→2)
    2. **daß** may be omitted. The verb in this case must stand in second position in the clause, instead of being placed at the end (→3)

Forms of the Subjunctive in Indirect Speech

See the conjugation of verbs in the subjunctive pp.8 to 15 and 26 to 31. In indirect (or reported) speech, wherever the present subjunctive is identical to the present indicative form, the imperfect subjunctive is used instead (→4)

1 **Er sagte: "Sie kennt deine Schwester"**
   He said, "She knows your sister"
   Er sagte, sie kenne meine Schwester
   He said she knew my sister
   "Habe ich zu viel gesagt?", fragte er
   "Did I say too much?", he asked
   Er fragte, ob er zuviel gesagt habe
   He asked if he had said too much

2 **Er hat uns gesagt, daß er Französisch spreche**
   He told us that he spoke French

3 **Er hat uns gesagt, er spreche Französisch**
   He told us he spoke French

4 PRESENT SUBJUNCTIVE IN INDIRECT SPEECH

   WEAK VERBS e.g. **holen** to fetch:

ich holte	wir holten
du holest	ihr holet
er hole	sie holten

   STRONG VERBS e.g. **singen** to sing:

ich sänge	wir sängen
du singest	ihr singet
er singe	sie sängen

Verbs with Prefixes

Many verbs in German begin with a prefix. A prefix is a word or part of a word which precedes the verb stem (→**1**)

- Often the addition of a prefix changes the meaning of the basic verb (→**2**)

- Prefixes may be found in strong, weak or mixed verbs. Adding a prefix may occasionally change the verb conjugation (→**3**)

- There are four kinds of prefix and each behaves in a slightly different way, as shown on the following pages. Prefixes may be:

  > inseparable (→**4**)

  > separable (→**5**)

  > double (→**6**)

  > variable, i.e. either separable or inseparable, depending on the verb (→**7**)

Continued

1 zu + geben = zugeben
an + ziehen = anziehen

2 nehmen to take
zunehmen to put on weight, to increase
sich benehmen to behave

3 WEAK: STRONG:
suchen   to look for   stehen   to stand
versuchen   to try   verstehen   to understand
besuchen   to visit   aufstehen   to get up

WEAK: WEAK:
löschen   to extinguish   fehlen   to be missing
STRONG: STRONG:
erlöschen   to go out   empfehlen   to recommend

4 entdecken to discover
er entdeckt, er entdeckte, er hat entdeckt

5 mitmachen to join in
er macht mit, er machte mit, er hat mitgemacht

6 ausverkaufen to sell off
er verkauft aus, er verkaufte aus, er hat ausverkauft

7 wiederholen to repeat
er wiederholt, er wiederholte, er hat wiederholt

wieder(-)holen to fetch back
er holt wieder, er holte wieder, er hat wiedergeholt

Verbs with Prefixes (ctd.)

Inseparable Prefixes

● The eight inseparable prefixes are:

be-	**emp-**
ge-	**ent-**
er-	**miß-**
ver-	**zer-** (→**1**)

● These exist only as prefixes, and cannot be words in their own right.

● They are never separated from the verb stem, whatever tense of the verb is used (→**2**)

● Inseparable prefixes are always unstressed (→**3**)

● They have no **ge-** in their past participles (see p.50) (→**4**)

Continued

1 **beschreiben**   to describe
   gehören   to belong
   erhalten   to contain
   verlieren   to lose
   empfangen   to receive
   enttäuschen   to disappoint
   mißtrauen   to mistrust
   zerlegen   to dismantle

2 **besuchen**   to visit:

   Er besucht uns regelmäßig
   He visits us regularly
   Er besuchte uns jeden Tag
   He used to visit us every day
   Er hat uns jeden Tag besucht
   He visited us every day
   Er wird uns morgen besuchen
   He will visit us tomorrow
   Besuche sofort deine Tante!
   Visit your aunt at once

3 **erlauben,   verstehen,   empfangen,   vergessen**

4 COMPARE:
   verstehen: wir haben verstanden we understood
   stehen: wir haben gestanden we stood

   empfangen: wir haben empfangen we received
   fangen: wir haben gefangen we caught

Verbs with Prefixes (ctd.)

Separable Prefixes

Some common examples are:

ab	empor	herbei	hinauf	nieder
an	entgegen	herein	hinaus	vor
auf	fest	herüber	hindurch	vorbei
aus	frei	herum	hinein	vorüber
bei	her	herunter	hinüber	weg
da(r)	herab	hervor	hinunter	zu
davon	heran	hierher	los	zurecht
dazu	herauf	hin	mit	zurück
ein	heraus	hinab	nach	zusammen

- Unlike inseparable prefixes, separable prefixes may be words in their own right. Indeed, nouns, adjectives, adverbs and even other verbs are often used as separable prefixes (→1)

- The past participle of a verb with a separable prefix is formed with **ge-**. It comes between the verb and the prefix (→2)

- In main clauses, the prefix is placed at the end of the clause if the verb is in a simple tense (i.e. present, imperfect or imperative form) (→3)

- In subordinate clauses, whatever the tense of the verb, the prefix is attached to the verb and the resulting whole placed at the end of the clause (→4)

- Where an infinitive construction requiring **zu** is used (see p.46), the **zu** is placed between the infinitive and prefix to form one word (→5)

1 *noun + verb*:   **teilnehmen** to take part
       verb + verb: **kennenlernen** to get to know
       adjective + verb: **loswerden** to get free of
       adverb + verb: **niederlegen** to lay down

2 **Er ist gestern spazierengegangen**
       He went for a walk yesterday
       Wir sind an der Grenze zurückgewiesen worden
       We were turned back at the border

3 **wegbringen**: to take for repair, to take away
       PRESENT: **Wir bringen das Auto weg**
       IMPERFECT: **Wir brachten das Auto weg**
       IMPERATIVE: **Bringt das Auto weg!**

       CONDITIONAL: **Wir würden das Auto wegbringen**
       FUTURE: **Wir werden das Auto wegbringen**
       PERFECT: **Wir haben das Auto weggebracht**
       PERFECT PASSIVE: **Das Auto ist weggebracht worden**
       PLUPERFECT SUBJUNCTIVE: **Wir hätten das Auto weggebracht**

4 PRESENT: **Weil wir das Auto wegbringen, ...**
       IMPERFECT: **Daß wir das Auto wegbrachten, ...**
       PERFECT: **Nachdem wir das Auto weggebracht haben, ...**
       PLUPERFECT SUBJUNCTIVE: **Wenn wir das Auto weggebracht hätten, ...**
       FUTURE: **Obwohl wir das Auto wegbringen werden, ...**

5 **Um das Auto rechtzeitig wegzubringen, müssen wir morgen früh aufstehen**
       In order to take the car in on time, we shall have to get up early

Verbs with Prefixes (ctd.)

Variable Prefixes

These are:

über	um
unter	voll
durch	wider
hinter	wieder

- These can be separable or inseparable (→1)

- Often they are used separably and inseparably with the same verb. In such cases the verb and prefix will tend to retain their basic meanings if the prefix is used separably, but adopt figurative meanings when the prefix is used inseparably (→2)

- Variable prefixes behave as separable prefixes when used separably, and as inseparable prefixes when used inseparably (→3)

Double Prefixes

These occur where a verb with an inseparable prefix is preceded by a separable prefix (→4)

- The separable prefix behaves as described on page 72, the verb plus inseparable prefix representing the basic verb to which the separable prefix is attached (→5)

- Unlike other separable verbs, however, verbs with double prefixes have no **ge-** in their past participles (→6)

1 **unternehmen** (*inseparable*) to undertake, take on:

   Wir haben in den Ferien vieles unternommen
   We did a great deal in the holidays
   Du unternimmst zuviel
   You take on too much

   untergehen (*separable*) to sink, go down:

   Die Sonne ist untergegangen
   The sun has gone down/has set
   Die Sonne geht unter
   The sun is going down/is setting

2 **etwas wiederholen** (*separable*) to retrieve something
   etwas wiederholen (*inseparable*) to repeat something

3 **Er holte ihr die Tasche wieder**
   He brought her back her bag
   Er wiederholte den Satz
   He repeated the sentence

4 **ausverkaufen** to sell off

5 **Er verkauft alles aus**
   He's selling everything off
   Um alles auszuverkaufen ...
   In order to sell everything off ...
   Er wird alles ausverkaufen
   He'll be selling everything off

6 **Er hat doch alles ausverkauft**
   But he's sold everything off

Verbs followed by Prepositions

- Some verbs in English usage require a preposition (*for*/*with*/*by* etc) for their completion.
  This also happens in German, though the prepositions used with German verbs may not be those expected from their English counterparts (→**1**)

- The preposition used may significantly alter the meaning of a verb in German (→**2**)

- Occasionally German verbs use a preposition where their English equivalents do not (→**3**)

- Prepositions used with verbs behave as normal prepositions and affect the *case* of the following noun (see p.198).

- A verb plus preposition may be followed by a clause containing another verb rather than by a noun or pronoun. This often corresponds to an -*ing* construction in English:
  Thank you for *coming*
  In German, this is dealt with in two ways:
  1. Where the "verb-plus-preposition" construction has the same subject as the following verb, the preposition is preceded by **da-** or **dar-** and the following verb becomes an infinitive used with **zu** (→**4**)
  2. Where the subject of the "verb-plus-preposition" is not the same as for the following verb, a **daß** clause is used (→**5**)

- Following clauses may also be introduced by interrogatives (**ob, wie** etc) if the meaning demands them (→**6**)

Continued

1   Compare:

GERMAN	ENGLISH
sich sehnen **nach**	to long *for*
warten **auf**	to wait *for*
bitten **um**	to ask *for*

2   **bestehen** to pass (an examination/test *etc*)
     bestehen aus to consist of
     bestehen auf to insist on

     sich freuen auf to look forward to
     sich freuen über to be pleased about

3   **diskutieren über** to discuss

4   **Ich freue mich sehr darauf, mal wieder mit ihm zu arbeiten**
     I am looking forward to working with him again

5   **Ich freue mich sehr darauf, daß du morgen kommst**
     I am looking forward to your coming tomorrow
     Er sorgte dafür, daß die Kinder immer gut gepflegt waren
     He saw to it that the children were always well cared for

6   **Er dachte lange darüber nach, ob er es wirklich kaufen**
     wollte
     He thought for ages about whether he really wanted to buy it
     Sie freut sich darüber, wie ihre Schüler so schnell gelernt
     haben
     She is pleased at how quickly her students have learned

Verbs followed by Prepositions (ctd.)

Common verbs followed by preposition + accusative case:
achten auf to pay attention to, keep an eye on (→1)
sich amüsieren über to laugh at, smile about
sich ärgern über to get annoyed about/with
sich bewerben um to apply for (→2)
bitten um to ask for (→3)
denken an to be thinking of (→4)
denken über to hold an opinion of, think about (→5)
sich erinnern an to remember
sich freuen auf to look forward to
sich freuen über to be pleased about (→6)
sich gewöhnen an to get used to (→7)
sich interessieren für to be interested in (→8)
kämpfen um to fight for
sich kümmern um to take care of, see to
nachdenken über to ponder, reflect on (→9)
sich unterhalten über to talk about
sich verlassen auf to rely on, depend on (→10)
warten auf to wait for

Common verbs followed by preposition + dative case:
abhängen von to be dependent on (→11)
sich beschäftigen mit to occupy oneself with (→12)
bestehen aus to consist of (→13)
leiden an/unter to suffer from (→14)
neigen zu to be inclined to
riechen nach to smell of (→15)
schmecken nach to taste of
sich sehnen nach to long for
sterben an to die of
teilnehmen an to take part in (→16)
träumen von to dream of (→17)
sich verabschieden von to say goodbye to
sich verstehen mit to get along with, get on with
zittern vor to tremble with (→18)

1 Er mußte auf die Kinder achten
He had to keep an eye on the children
2 Sie hat sich um die Stelle als Buchhalterin beworben
She applied for the post of book-keeper
3 Die Kinder baten ihre Mutter um Plätzchen
The children asked their mother for some biscuits
4 Woran denkst du? What are you thinking about?
Daran habe ich gar nicht mehr gedacht
I'd forgotten about that
5 Wie denkt ihr darüber? What do you think about it?
6 Ich freute mich sehr darüber, Johann besucht zu haben
I was very glad I had visited Johann
7 Man gewöhnt sich an alles One gets used to anything
8 Sie interessiert sich sehr für Politik
She is very interested in politics
9 Er hatte schon lange darüber nachgedacht
He had been thinking about it for a long time
10 Er verläßt sich darauf, daß seine Frau alles tut
He relies on his wife to do everything
11 Das hängt davon ab It all depends
12 Sie sind im Moment sehr damit beschäftigt, ihr neues Haus in Ordnung zu bringen
They are very busy sorting out their new house at the moment
13 Dieser Kuchen besteht aus Eiern, Mehl und Zucker
This cake consists of eggs, flour and sugar
14 Sie hat lange an dieser Krankheit gelitten
She suffered from this illness for a long time
Alte Leute können sehr unter der Einsamkeit leiden
Old people can suffer dreadful loneliness
15 Der Kuchen hat nach Zimt gerochen
The cake smelled of cinnamon
16 Sie hat an der Bonner Tagung teilnehmen müssen
She had to attend the Bonn conference
17 Er hat von seinem Urlaub geträumt
He dreamt of his holiday
18 Er zitterte vor Freude He was trembling with joy

Verbs followed by the Dative

Some verbs have a direct object and an indirect object. In the English sentence *He gave me a book*, *me* (= *to me*) is the indirect object and would appear in the dative case in German; *a book* is the direct object of *gave* and would be in the accusative (→1)

● In German, as in English, this type of verb is usually concerned with giving or telling something to someone, or with performing an action for someone (→2)

● The normal word order after such verbs is for the direct object to follow the indirect, *except* where the direct object is a personal pronoun (see p.224) (→2)
This order may be reversed for emphasis (→3)

● Some examples of verbs followed by the dative in this way:

anbieten	bringen	beweisen
erzählen	geben	gönnen
kaufen	leihen	mitteilen
schenken	schicken	schulden
schreiben	verkaufen	zeigen (→4)

● Certain verbs in German however can be followed *only* by an indirect object in the dative case. These should be noted especially, since most of them are quite different from their English equivalents:

begegnen	danken	fehlen
gefallen	gehören	gelingen
gleichen	gratulieren	helfen
imponieren	mißtrauen	nachgehen
schaden	schmecken	schmeicheln
trauen	trotzen	vorangehen
weh tun	widersprechen	widerstehen (→5)

● For how to form the passive of such verbs, see p.36.

1 **Er gab mir ein Buch** He gave me a book

2 **Er wusch dem Kind** (*indirect*) **das Gesicht** (*direct*)
He washed the child's face
Er erzählte ihm (*indirect*) **eine Geschichte** (*direct*)
He told him a story
BUT
Er hat sie (*direct*) **meiner Mutter** (*indirect*) **gezeigt**
He showed it to my mother
Kaufst du es (*direct*) **mir** (*indirect*)?
Will you buy it for me?

3 **Er wollte das Buch** (*dir.*) **seiner Mutter** (*indir.*) **geben**
(*This emphasises* **seiner Mutter**)
He wanted to give the book to his mother

4 **Er bot ihr den Zucker an** He offered her the sugar
Bringst du mir eins? Will you bring me one?
Ich gönne dir das neue Kleid
I want you to have the new dress
Er hat ihr mitgeteilt, daß ... He told her that ...
Ich schenke meiner Mutter Parfüm zum Geburtstag
I am giving my mother perfume for her birthday
Das schulde ich ihm I owe him that
Zeig es mir! Show me it!

6 **Er ist seinem Freund in der Stadt begegnet**
He bumped into his friend in town
Mir fehlt den Mut dazu I don't have the courage
Es ist ihnen gelungen They succeeded
Wem gehört dieses Buch? Whose book is this?
Er wollte ihr nicht helfen He refused to help her
Ich gratuliere dir! Congratulations!
Rauchen schadet der Gesundheit!
Smoking is bad for your health
Das Essen hat ihnen gut geschmeckt
They enjoyed the meal

There is/There are

There are three ways of expressing this in German:

es gibt

- This is always used in the singular form, and is followed by an accusative object which may be either singular or plural (→1)
- **es gibt** is used to refer to things of a general nature or location (→2)
- It also has some idiomatic usages (→3)

es ist/es sind

- The **es** here merely introduces the real subject. The verb therefore becomes plural where the real subject is plural. the real subject is in the nominative case (→4)
- The **es** is not required and is therefore omitted when the verb and real subject come together. This happens when inversion of subject and verb occurs (see p.226) and in subordinate clauses (→5)
- **es ist** or **es sind** are used to refer to
    1. subjects with a specific and confined location. This location must always be mentioned either by name or by **da, darauf, darin** etc (→6)
    2. temporary existence (→7)
    3. as a beginning to a story (→8)

The Passive Voice

Often *there is/there are* in English will be rendered by a verb in the passive voice in German (→9)

1 Es gibt zu viele Probleme dabei
There are too many problems involved
Es gibt kein Besseres bier
There's no better beer

2 Es gibt bestimmt Regen
It's definitely going to rain
Ruhe hat es bei uns nie gegeben
There has never been any peace here

3 Was gibt's (= gibt es) zum Essen? What's there to eat?
Was gibt's? What's wrong? What's up?
So was gibt's doch nicht! That's impossible!

4 Es waren zwei ältere Leute unten im Hof
There were two elderly people down in the yard
Es sind so viele Touristen da
There are so many tourists there

5 Unten im Hof waren zwei ältere Leute
Down in the yard were two elderly people
Wenn so viele Touristen da sind ...
If there are so many tourists there ...

6 Es waren viele Flaschen Sekt im Keller
There were a lot of bottles of champagne in the cellar
**Ein Brief lag auf dem Tisch. Es waren auch zwei Bücher
darauf**
A letter lay on the table. There were also two books on it

7 Es war niemand da There was no-one there

8 Es war einmal ein König ...
Once upon a time there was a king ...

9 Es wurde auf der Party viel getrunken
There was a lot of drinking at the party

Use of "es" as an anticipatory object

Many verbs can have as their object a **daß** clause or an infinitive with **zu** (→1)

- With some verbs **es** is used as an object to anticipate this clause or infinitive phrase (→2)
- When the clause or infinitive phrase begins the sentence, **es** is not used in the main clause but its place may be taken by an optional **das** (→3)

Common verbs which usually have the "es" object

es ablehnen, zu to refuse to
es aushalten, zu tun/daß to stand doing (→4)
es ertragen, zu tun/daß to endure doing
es leicht haben, zu to find it easy to (→5)
es nötig haben, zu to need to (→6)
es satt haben, zu to have had enough of (doing)
es verstehen, zu to know how to (→7)

Common verbs which often have the "es" object

es jemandem anhören/ansehen, daß to tell by listening to/looking at somone that (→8)
es begreifen, daß/warum/wie to understand that/why/how
es bereuen, zu tun/daß to regret having done/that
es leugnen, daß to deny that (→9)
es unternehmen, zu to undertake to
es jemandem verbieten, zu to forbid someone to
es jemandem vergeben, daß to forgive someone for (doing)
es jemandem verschweigen, daß not to tell someone that
es jemandem verzeihen, daß to forgive someone for (doing)
es wagen zu to dare to

1 **Er wußte, daß wir pünktlich kommen würden**
He knew that we would come on time
Sie fing an zu lachen
She began to laugh

2 **Er hatte es abgelehnt mitzufahren**
He had refused to come

3 **Daß es Peter war, das haben wir ihr verschwiegen**
OR: **Daß es Peter war, haben wir ihr verschwiegen**
We didn't tell her that it was Peter

4 **Ich halte es nicht mehr aus, bei ihnen zu arbeiten**
I can't stand working for them any longer

5 **Er hatte es nicht leicht, sie zu überreden**
He didn't have an easy job persuading them

6 **Ich habe es nicht nötig, mit dir darüber zu reden**
I don't have to talk to you about it

7 **Er versteht es, Autos zu reparieren**
He knows about repairing cars

8 **Man hörte es ihm sofort an, daß er kein Deutscher war**
OR: **Daß er kein Deutscher war, (das) hörte man ihm sofort an**
One could tell immediately (from the way he spoke) that he wasn't German

Man sieht es ihm sofort an, daß er dein Bruder ist
OR: **Daß er dein Bruder ist, (das) sieht man ihm sofort an**
One can tell at a glance that he's your brother

9 **Er hat es nie geleugnet, das Geld genommen zu haben**
He has never denied taking the money

Strong and Mixed Verbs - Principal Parts

INFINITIVE		3RD PERSON PRESENT
backen	to bake	er bäckt
befehlen	to command	er befiehlt
beginnen	to begin	er beginnt
beißen	to bite	er beißt
bergen	to rescue	er birgt
bersten	to burst *intr*	er birst
betrügen	to deceive	er betrügt
biegen	to bend *tr*/to turn *intr*	er biegt
bieten	to offer	er bietet
binden	to tie	er bindet
bitten	to ask for	er bittet
blasen	to blow	er bläst
bleiben	to remain	er bleibt
braten	to fry	er brät
brechen	to break	er bricht
brennen	to burn	er brennt
bringen	to bring	er bringt
denken	to think	er denkt
dreschen	to thresh	er drischt
dringen	to penetrate	er dringt
dürfen	to be allowed to	er darf
empfehlen	to recommend	er empfiehlt
erlöschen	to go out (*fire, light*)	er erlischt
erschallen	to resound	er erschallt
erschrecken	to be startled[1]	er erschrickt
erwägen	to weigh up	er erwägt
essen	to eat	er ißt
fahren	to travel	er fährt

1. **erschrecken** meaning "to frighten" is **weak**:
   erschrecken, erschreckt, erschreckte, hat erschreckt

3RD PERSON IMPERFECT	PERFECT	IMPERFECT SUBJUNCTIVE
er backte	er hat gebacken	er backte
er befahl	er hat befohlen	er befähle
er begann	er hat begonnen	er begänne
er biß	er hat gebissen	er bisse
er barg	er hat geborgen	er bärge
er barst	er ist geborsten	er bärste
er betrog	er hat betrogen	er betröge
er bog	er hat/ist gebogen	er böge
er bot	er hat geboten	er böte
er band	er hat gebunden	er bände
er bat	er hat gebeten	er bäte
er blies	er hat geblasen	er bliese
er blieb	er ist geblieben	er bliebe
er briet	er hat gebraten	er briete
er brach	er hat/ist gebrochen	er bräche
er brannte	er hat gebrannt	er brennte
er brachte	er hat gebracht	er brächte
er dachte	er hat gedacht	er dächte
er drosch	er hat gedroschen	er drösche
er drang	er ist gedrungen	er dränge
er durfte	er hat gedurft/dürfen[1]	er dürfte
er empfahl	er hat empfohlen	er empfähle
er erlosch	er ist erloschen	er erlösche
er erschallte	er ist erschollen	er erschölle
er erschrak	er ist erschrocken	er erschräke
er erwog	er hat erwogen	er erwöge
er aß	er hat gegessen	er äße
er fuhr	er ist gefahren	er führe

1. The second (infinitive) form is used when combined with an infinitive construction (see p.56).

Continued

INFINITIVE		3RD PERSON PRESENT
fallen	to fall	er fällt
fangen	to catch	er fängt
fechten	to fight	er ficht
fliegen	to fly	er fliegt
fliehen	to flee *tr/intr*	er flieht
fließen	to flow	er fließt
fressen	to eat (*of animals*)	er frißt
frieren	to be cold; freeze over	er friert
gebären	to give birth to	sie gebärt
geben	to give	er gibt
gedeihen	to thrive	er gedeiht
gehen	to go	er geht
gelingen	to succeed	es gelingt
gelten	to be valid	er gilt
genesen	to get well	er genest
genießen	to enjoy	er genießt
geraten	to get into (*a state etc*)	er gerät
geschehen	to happen	er geschieht
gewinnen	to win	er gewinnt
gießen	to pour	er gießt
gleichen	to resemble; equal	er gleicht
gleiten	to glide	er gleitet
glimmen	to glimmer	er glimmt
graben	to dig	er gräbt
greifen	to grip	er greift
haben	to have	er hat
halten	to hold, stop	er hält
hängen	to hang *intr*[1]	er hängt
heben	to lift	er hebt
heißen	to be called	er heißt

1. **hängen** is **weak** when used transitively.

3RD PERSON IMPERFECT	PERFECT	IMPERFECT SUBJUNCTIVE
er fiel	er ist gefallen	er fiele
er fing	er hat gefangen	er finge
er focht	er hat gefochten	er föchte
er flog	er hat/ist geflogen	er flöge
er floh	er hat/ist geflohen	er flöhe
er floß	er ist geflossen	er flösse
er fraß	er hat gefressen	er fräße
er fror	er hat/ist gefroren	er fröre
sie gebar	sie hat geboren	sie gebäre
er gab	er hat gegeben	er gäbe
er gedieh	er ist gediehen	er gediehe
er ging	er ist gegangen	er ginge
es gelang	es ist gelungen	es gelänge
er galt	er hat gegolten	er gälte
er genas	er ist genesen	er genäse
er genoß	er hat genossen	er genösse
er geriet	er ist geraten	er geriete
er geschah	er ist geschehen	er geschähe
er gewann	er ist gewonnen	er gewönne
er goß	er hat gegossen	er gösse
er glich	er hat geglichen	er gliche
er glitt	er ist geglitten	er glitte
er glomm	er hat geglommen	er glömme
er grub	er hat gegraben	er grübe
er griff	er hat gegriffen	er griffe
er hatte	er hat gehabt	er hätte
er hielt	er hat gehalten	er hielte
er hing	er hat gehangen	er hinge
er hob	er hat gehoben	er höbe
er hieß	er hat geheißen	er hieße

Continued

INFINITIVE		3RD PERSON PRESENT
helfen	to help	**er hilft**
kennen	to know (*someone etc*)	**er kennt**
klingen	to sound	**er klingt**
kommen	to come	**er kommt**
kneifen	to pinch	**er kneift**
können	to be able to	**er kann**
kriechen	to crawl	**er kriecht**
laden	to load	**er lädt**
lassen	to allow	**er läßt**
laufen	to walk; run	**er läuft**
leiden	to suffer	**er leidet**
leihen	to lend	**er leiht**
lesen	to read	**er liest**
liegen	to lie	**er liegt**
lügen	to tell a lie	**er lügt**
mahlen	to grind	**er mahlt**
messen	to measure	**er mißt**
mißlingen	to fail	**es mißlingt**
mögen	to like to	**er mag**
müssen	to have to	**er muß**
nehmen	to take	**er nimmt**
nennen	to call	**er nennt**
pfeifen	to whistle	**er pfeift**
preisen	to praise	**er preist**
quellen	to gush	**er quillt**
raten	to advise; guess	**er rät**
reiben	to rub	**er reibt**
reißen	to tear *tr/intr*	**er reißt**
reiten	to ride *tr/intr*	**er reitet**

3RD PERSON IMPERFECT	PERFECT	IMPERFECT SUBJUNCTIVE
er half	er hat geholfen	er hülfe
er kannte	er hat gekannt	er kennte
er klang	er hat geklungen	er klänge
er kam	er ist gekommen	er käme
er kniff	er hat gekniffen	er kniffe
er konnte	er hat gekonnt/können[1]	er könnte
er kroch	er ist gekrochen	er kröche
er lud	er hat geladen	er lüde
er ließ	er hat gelassen	er ließe
er lief	er ist gelaufen	er liefe
er litt	er hat gelitten	er litte
er lieh	er hat geliehen	er liehe
er las	er hat gelesen	er läse
er lag	er hat gelegen	er läge
er log	er hat gelogen	er löge
er mahlte	er hat gemahlen	er mahlte
er maß	er hat gemessen	er mäße
es mißlang	es ist mißlungen	es mißlänge
er mochte	er hat gemocht/mögen[1]	er möchte
er mußte	er hat gemußt/müssen[1]	er müßte
er nahm	er hat genommen	er nähme
er nannte	er hat genannt	er nennte
er pfiff	er hat gepfiffen	er pfiffe
er pries	er hat gepriesen	er priese
er quoll	er ist gequollen	er quölle
er riet	er hat geraten	er riete
er rieb	er hat gerieben	er riebe
er riß	er hat/ist gerissen	er risse
er ritt	er hat/ist geritten	er ritte

1. The second (infinitive) form is used when combined with an infinitive construction (see p.56).

Continued

INFINITIVE		3RD PERSON PRESENT
rennen	to run	**er rennt**
riechen	to smell	**er riecht**
ringen	to wrestle	**er ringt**
rinnen	to flow	**er rinnt**
rufen	to shout	**er ruft**
salzen	to salt	**er salzt**
saufen	to booze; drink	**er säuft**
saugen	to suck	**er saugt**
schaffen	to create[1]	**er schafft**
scheiden	to separate *tr/intr*	**er scheidet**
scheinen	to seem; shine	**er scheint**
schelten	to scold	**er schilt**
scheren	to shear	**er schert**
schieben	to shove	**er schiebt**
schießen	to shoot	**er schießt**
schlafen	to sleep	**er schläft**
schlagen	to hit	**er schlägt**
schleichen	to creep	**er schleicht**
schleifen	to grind	**er schleift**
schließen	to close	**er schließt**
schlingen	to wind	**er schlingt**
schmeißen	to fling	**er schmeißt**
schmelzen	to melt *tr/intr*	**er schmilzt**
schneiden	to cut	**er schneidet**
schreiben	to write	**er schreibt**
schreien	to shout	**er schreit**
schreiten	to stride	**er schreitet**
schweigen	to be silent	**er schweigt**

1. **schaffen** meaning "to work hard/manage" is **weak**:
   schaffen, schafft, schaffte, hat geschafft

3RD PERSON IMPERFECT	PERFECT	IMPERFECT SUBJUNCTIVE
er rannte	er ist gerannt	er rennte
er roch	er hat gerochen	er röche
er rang	er hat gerungen	er ränge
er rann	er ist geronnen	er ränne
er rief	er hat gerufen	er riefe
er salzte	er hat gesalzen	er salzte
er soff	er hat gesoffen	er söffe
er sog	er hat gesogen	er söge
er schuf	er hat geschaffen	er schüfe
er schied	er hat/ist geschieden	er schiede
er schien	er hat geschienen	er schiene
er schalt	er hat gescholten	er schölte
er schor	er hat geschoren	er schöre
er schob	er hat geschoben	er schöbe
er schoß	er hat geschossen	er schösse
er schlief	er hat geschlafen	er schliefe
er schlug	er hat geschlagen	er schlüge
er schlich	er ist geschlichen	er schliche
er schliff	er hat geschliffen	er schliffe
er schloß	er hat geschlossen	er schlösse
er schlang	er hat geschlungen	er schlänge
er schmiß	er hat geschmissen	er schmisse
er schmolz	er hat/ist geschmolzen	er schmölze
er schnitt	er hat geschnitten	er schnitte
er schrieb	er hat geschrieben	er schriebe
er schrie	er hat geschrieen	er schriee
er schritt	er ist geschritten	er schritte
er schwieg	er hat geschwiegen	er schwiege

Continued

INFINITIVE

3RD PERSON
PRESENT

schwellen	to swell *intr*[1]	er schwillt
schwimmen	to swim	er schwimmt
schwingen	to swing	er schwingt
schwören	to vow	er schwört
sehen	to see	er sieht
sein	to be	er ist
senden	to send[2]	er sendet
singen	to sing	er singt
sinken	to sink	er sinkt
sinnen	to ponder	er sinnt
sitzen	to sit	er sitzt
sollen	to be supposed to be	er soll
spalten	to split *tr/intr*	er spaltet
speien	to spew	er speit
spinnen	to spin	er spinnt
sprechen	to speak	er spricht
sprießen	to sprout	er sprießt
springen	to jump	er springt
stechen	to sting/prick	er sticht
stehen	to stand	er steht
stehlen	to steal	er stiehlt
steigen	to climb	er steigt
sterben	to die	er stirbt
stinken	to stink	er stinkt
stoßen	to knock/come across	er stießt
streichen	to stroke/wander	er streicht
streiten	to quarrel	er streitet

1. **schwellen** is weak when used transitively:
   schwellen, schwellt, schwellte, hat geschwellt
2. **senden** meaning "to broadcast" is weak:
   senden, sendet, sendete, hat gesendet

3RD PERSON IMPERFECT	PERFECT	IMPERFECT SUBJUNCTIVE
er schwoll	er ist geschwollen	er schwölle
er schwam	er ist geschwommen	er schwömme
er schwang	er hat geschwungen	er schwänge
er schwor	er hat geschworen	er schwüre
er sah	er hat gesehen	er sähe
er war	er ist gewesen	er wäre
er sandte	er hat gesandt	er sendete
er sang	er hat gesungen	er sänge
er sank	er hat gesunken	er sänke
er sann	er hat gesonnen	er sänne
er saß	er hat gesessen	er säße
er sollte	er hat gesollt/sollen[1]	er sollte
er spaltete	er hat/ist gespalten	er spaltete
er spie	er hat gespieen	er spiee
er spann	er hat gesponnen	er spönne
er sprach	er hat gesprochen	er spräche
er sproß	er ist gesprossen	er sprösse
er sprang	er ist gesprungen	er spränge
er stach	er hat gestochen	er stäche
er stand	er hat gestanden	er stünde
er stahl	er hat gestohlen	er stähle
er stieg	er ist gestiegen	er stiege
er starb	er ist gestorben	er stürbe
er stank	er hat gestunken	er stänke
er stieß	er hat/ist gestoßen	er stieße
er strich	er hat/ist gestrichen	er striche
er stritt	er hat gestritten	er stritte

1. The second (infinitive) form is used when combined with an infinitive construction (see p.56).

Continued

INFINITIVE		3RD PERSON PRESENT
tragen	to carry; wear	er trägt
treffen	to meet	er trifft
treiben	to drive; engage in	er treibt
treten	to kick/step	er tritt
trinken	to drink	er trinkt
tun	to do	er tut
verderben	to spoil/go bad	er verdirbt
verdrießen	to irritate	er verdrießt
vergessen	to forget	er vergißt
verlieren	to lose	er verliert
vermeiden	to avoid	er vermeidet
verschwinden	to disappear	er verschwindet
verzeihen	to pardon	er verzeiht
wachsen	to grow	er wächst
waschen	to wash	er wäscht
weichen	to yield	er weicht
weisen	to point	er weist
wenden	to turn	er wendet
werben	to recruit	er wirbt
werden	to become	er wird
werfen	to throw	er wirft
wiegen	to weigh[1]	er wiegt
winden	to wind	er windet
wissen	to know	er weiß
wollen	to want to	er will
ziehen	to pull	er zieht
zwingen	to force	er zwingt

1. **wiegen** meaning "to rock" is **weak**

3RD PERSON IMPERFECT	PERFECT	IMPERFECT SUBJUNCTIVE
er trug	er hat getragen	er trüge
er traf	er hat getroffen	er träfe
er trieb	er hat getrieben	er triebe
er trat	er hat/ist getreten	er träte
er trank	er hat getrunken	er tränke
er tat	er hat getan	er täte
er verdarb	er hat/ist verdorben	er verdürbe
er verdroß	er hat verdrossen	er verdrösse
er vergaß	er hat vergessen	er vergäße
er verlor	er hat verloren	er verlöre
er vermied	er hat vermieden	er vermiede
er verschwand	er ist verschwunden	er verschwände
er verzieh	er hat verziehen	er verziehe
er wuchs	er ist gewachsen	er wüchse
er wusch	er hat gewaschen	er wüsche
er wich	er ist gewichen	er wiche
er wies	er hat gewiesen	er wiese
er wandte	er hat gewandt	er wendete
er warb	er hat geworben	er würbe
er wurde	er ist geworden	er würde
er warf	er hat geworfen	er würfe
er wog	er hat gewogen	er wöge
er wand	er hat gewunden	er wände
er wußte	er hat gewußt	er wüßte
er wollte	er hat gewollt/wollen[1]	er wollte
er zog	er hat gezogen	er zöge
er zwang	er hat gezwungen	er zwänge

1. The second (infinitive) form is used when combined with an infinitive construction (see p.56).

The Declension of Nouns

In German, all nouns may be declined. This means that they may change their form according to their

> *gender* (i.e. masculine, feminine or neuter) (→**1**)
>
> *case* (i.e. their function in the sentence) (→**2**)
>
> *number* (i.e. singular or plural) (→**3**)

- Nearly all *feminine* nouns change in the *plural* form by adding **-n** or **-en**. Many *masculine* and *neuter* nouns also change (→**4**)

- *Masculine* and *neuter* nouns, with a few exceptions, add **-s** (**-s** or **-es** for nouns of one syllable) in the *genitive singular* (but see p.110) (→**5**)

- All nouns end in **-n** or **-en** in the *dative plural*. This is added to the nominative plural form, where this does not already end in **-n** (→**6**)

- A good dictionary will provide guidance in how to decline a noun:
  The nominative singular form is given in full, followed by the gender of the noun, then the genitive singular and nominative plural endings are shown where appropriate (→**7**)

- Adjectives used as nouns are declined as adjectives rather than nouns. Their declension endings are therefore dictated by the preceding article, as well as by number, case and gender (see p.140) (→**8**)

Continued

1 der Tisch (*masculine*) the table
  die Gabel (*feminine*) the fork
  das Mädchen (*neuter*) the girl

2 des Tisches of the table
  auf den Tischen on the tables

3 die Tische the tables
  die Gabeln the forks
  die Mädchen the girls

4

	NOM. SING.	NOM. PLURAL
MASC	der Apfel	die Äpfel
FEM	die Schule	die Schulen
NEUT	das Kind	die Kinder

5

	NOM. SING.	GEN. SING.
MASC	der Apfel	des Apfels
FEM	die Schule	der Schule
NEUT	das Kind	des Kind(e)s

6 den Äpfeln
  den Schulen
  den Kindern

7 Tiger *m* —s, —

NOM. SING.	der Tiger	the tiger
GEN. SING.	des Tigers	of the tiger, the tiger's
NOM. PL.	die Tiger	the tigers

8 der Angestellte   the employee
  ein Angestellter   an employee
  (die) Angestellten   (the) employees

The Gender of Nouns

In German a noun may be masculine, feminine or neuter. Gender is relatively unpredictable and has to be learned for each noun. This is best done by learning each noun with its definite article, i.e.

der Teppich, die Zeit, das Bild

The following are intended therefore only as guidelines in helping decide the gender of a word.

● Nouns denoting male people and animals are masculine (→1)

● Nouns denoting the female of the species, as shown on p.104 are of course feminine (→2)

● But nouns denoting an entire species can be of any gender (→3)

● Makes of cars identify with **der Wagen** and so are usually masculine (→4)

● Makes of aeroplane usually identify with **die Maschine** and so are feminine (→5)

● Seasons, months, days of the week, weather features and north, south, east, west are masculine (→6)

● Names of objects that perform an action are usually masculine (→7)

● Foreign nouns ending in **-ant, -ast, -ismus, -or** are masculine (→8) (But see the list of exceptions below)

● Nouns ending in **-ich, -ig, -ing, -ling** are masculine (→9)

Continued

1 **der Hörer** (male) listener
  der Löwe (male) lion
  der Onkel uncle
  der Vetter (male) cousin

2 **die Hörerin** (female) listener
  die Löwin lioness
  die Tante aunt
  die Kusine (female) cousin

3 **der Hund** dog
  die Schlange snake
  das Vieh cattle

4 **der Mercedes** Mercedes
  der VW Volkswagen

5 **die Boeing** Boeing
  die Concorde Concorde

6 **der Sommer** summer
  der Winter winter
  der August August
  der Freitag Friday
  der Wind wind
  der Schnee snow
  der Norden north
  der Osten east

7 **der Wecker** alarm clock
  der Computer computer

8 **der Ballast** ballast
  der Chauvinismus chauvinism

9 **der Essig** vinegar
  der Schmetterling butterfly

The Gender of Nouns (ctd.)

- Cardinal numbers are mostly feminine, but fractions are neuter (→**1**)

- Most nouns ending in **-e** are feminine (→**2**)
  EXCEPTIONS: male people or animals are masculine (→**3**)
  nouns beginning with **Ge-** are normally neuter (→**4**)

- Nouns ending in **-heit**, **-keit**, **-schaft**, **-ung**, **-ei** are feminine (→**5**)

- Foreign nouns ending in **-anz**, **-enz**, **-ie**, **-ik**, **-ion**, **-tät**, **-ur** are generally feminine (→**6**)

- Nouns denoting the young of a species are neuter (→**7**)

- Infinitives used as nouns are neuter (→**8**)

- Most nouns beginning with **Ge-** are neuter (→**9**)

- **-chen** or **-lein** may be added to many words to give a diminutive form. These words are then neuter (→**10**)
  Note that the vowel adds an umlaut where possible (i.e. on **a**, **o**, **u** or **au**) and a final **-e** is dropped before these endings (→**11**)

- Nouns ending in **-nis** or **-tum** are neuter (→**12**)

- Foreign nouns ending in **-at**, **-ett**, **-fon**, **-ma**, **-ment**, **-um**, **-ium** are mainly neuter (→**13**)

- Adjectives and participles may be used as masculine, feminine or neuter nouns (see p.148) (→**14**)

Continued

1 Er hat eine Drei gekriegt He got a three (*mark*)
  ein Drittel davon a third of it
2 die Falte crease, wrinkle
  die Brücke bridge
3 der Löwe lion
  der Matrose sailor
4 das Getreide crops
  das Gelände terrain, grounds
5 die Eitelkeit vanity
  die Gewerkschaft trade union
  die Scheidung divorce
  die Druckerei printing works
6 die Distanz distance
  die Konkurrenz rivalry
  die Theorie theory
  die Panik panic
  die Union union
  die Elektrizität electricity
  die Partitur score (*musical*)
7 das Baby baby
  das Kind child
8 das Schwimmen swimming
9 das Geschirr crockery, dishes
  das Geschöpf creature
10 das Kindlein child
11 das Fräulein young lady (*from* **die Frau**)
  das Kätzchen kitten (*from* **die Katze**)
12 das Ereignis event
  das Altertum antiquity
13 das Tablett tray
  das Telefon telephone
  das Testament will
  das Podium platform, podium
14 der Verwandte male relative
  die Verwandte female relative
  die Neuen new things

The Gender of Nouns

The following are some common exceptions to the gender guidelines shown on pp.100 to 103

> **das Weib** woman, wife
> **die Person** person
> **die Waise** orphan
> **das Mitglied** member
> **das Genie** genius
> **die Wache** sentry, guard
> **das Restaurant** restaurant

The Formation of Feminine Nouns

As in English, male and female forms are sometimes shown by two completely different words, e.g.
> *mother/father, uncle/aunt etc* (**→1**)

Where such separate forms do not exist, however, German often differentiates between male and female forms in one of two ways:

- The masculine form may sometimes be made feminine by the addition of **-in** in the singular and **-innen** in the plural (**→2**)

- An adjective may be used as a feminine noun (see p.148). It has feminine adjective endings which change according to the article which precedes it (see p.140) (**→3**)

Continued

1 **der Vater**   **die Mutter**
   father   mother
   der Bulle   **die Kuh**
   bull   cow
   der Mann   **die Frau**
   man   woman

2 **der Lehrer**   **die Lehrerin**
   (male) teacher   (female) teacher
   der König   **die Königin**
   king   queen
   der Hörer   **die Hörerin**
   (male) listener   (female) listener

   HENCE:
   Liebe Hörer und Hörerinnen! Dear listeners!
   unsere Leser und Leserinnen our readers

3 **eine Deutsche** a German woman
   Er ist mit einer Deutschen verheiratet
   He is married to a German
   die Abgeordnete the female MP
   Nur Abgeordnete durften dabeisein
   Only MP's were allowed in

The Gender of Nouns: miscellaneous points

Compound Nouns

Compound nouns, i.e. nouns composed of two or more nouns put together, are a regular feature of German.

- They normally take their gender and declension from the last noun of the compound word (→**1**)

- Exceptions to this are compounds ending in **-mut, -scheu** and **-wort**, which do not always have the same gender as the last word when it stands alone (→**2**)

Nouns with more than one gender

- A few nouns have two genders, either of which is acceptable (→**3**)

- Other nouns have two genders, each of which gives the noun a different meaning. (→**4**)

Abbreviations

- These take the gender of their principal noun (→**5**)

1 die **Armbanduhr** wristwatch (*from* die **Uhr**)
   der **Tomatensalat** tomato salad (*from* der **Salat**)
   der **Schlagzeugspieler** percussionist (*from* der **Spieler**)

2 der **Mut** courage
   die **Armut** poverty
   die **Demut** humility

   die **Scheu** fear, shyness, timidity
   der **Abscheu** repugnance, abhorrence

   das **Wort** word
   die **Antwort** reply

3 das/der **Radio** radio
   das/der **Keks** biscuit

4 der **Band** volume, book
   das **Band** ribbon, band, tape, bond
   der **See** lake
   die **See** sea
   der **Leiter** leader, manager
   die **Leiter** ladder
   der **Tau** dew
   das **Tau** rope, hawser

5 die **DDR** the German Democratic Republic (*from* die **Deutsche
   Demokratische Republik**)
   die **BRD** the Federal Republic of Germany (*from* die
   Bundesrepublik Deutschland)
   die **EG** the EEC (*from* die **Europäische Gemeinschaft**)

The Cases

There are four grammatical *cases*, which are generally shown by the form of the article used before the noun (see p.118).

The nominative case

● The nominative singular is the form shown in full in dictionary entries. The nominative plural is formed as described on p.98.

● The nominative case is used for:
— the subject of a verb (→**1**)
— the complement of **sein** or **werden** (→**2**)

The accusative case

● The noun in the accusative case usually has the same form as in the nominative (→**3**)
Exceptions to this are "weak" masculine nouns (see p.115) and adjectives used as nouns (see p.148).

● It is used:
— for the direct object of the verb (→**4**)
— after those prepositions which always take the accusative case (see p.206ff) (→**5**)
— to show change of location after prepositions of place (see p. 210) (→**6**)
— in many expressions of time and place which do not contain a preposition (→**7**)
— in certain fixed expressions (→**8**)

Continued

1 **Das Mädchen singt** The girl is singing

2 **Er ist ein guter Lehrer** He's a good teacher
   Das wird ein Pullover It's going to be a jumper

3 **das Lied** the song (*nominative*)
   das Lied the song (*accusative*)
   der Wagen the car (*nominative*)
   den Wagen the car (*accusative*)
   die Dose the tin (*nominative*)
   die Dose the tin (*accusative*)

4 **Er hat ein Lied gesungen** He sang a song

5 **für seine Freundin** for his girlfriend
   ohne diesen Wagen without this car
   durch das Rauchen through smoking

6 **in die Stadt** (*accusative*) into town
   BUT:
   in der Stadt (*dative*) in town

7 **Das macht sie jeden Donnerstag**
   She does that every Thursday
   Die Schule ist eine Kilometer entfernt
   The school is a kilometer away

8 **Guten Abend!** Good evening!
   Vielen Dank! Thank you very much!

The Cases (ctd.)

The genitive case

● In the genitive singular, *masculine* and *neuter* nouns take endings as follows:
  1) **-s** is added to nouns ending in **-en, -el, -er** (→**1**)
  2) **-es** is added to nouns ending in **-tz, -sch, -st** or **-ß** (→**2**)
  3) For nouns of one syllable, either **-s** or **-es** may be added (→**3**)

● *Feminine singular* and all *plural* nouns have the same form as their nominative.

● The genitive is used:
  — to show possession   (→**3**)
  — after prepositions taking the genitive (see p.212) (→**4**)
  — in expressions of time when the exact occasion is not specified (→**5**)

The dative case

● Singular nouns in the dative have the same form as in the nominative (→**6**)

● **-e** may be added to the dative singular of *masculine* and *neuter* nouns if the sentence rhythm needs it (→**7**)
  This **-e** is always used in certain set phrases (→**8**)

● Dative plural forms for all genders end in **-n** (→**9**)
  The only exceptions to this are some nouns of foreign origin that end in **-s** in all plural forms, including the dative plural (see p.114) (→**10**)

● The dative is used:
  — as the indirect object   (→**11**)
  — after verbs taking the dative (see p.80) (→**12**)
  — after prepositions taking the dative (see p.202) (→**13**)
  — in certain idiomatic expressions (→**14**)
  — instead of the possessive adjective to refer to parts of the body and items of clothing (see p.122) (→**15**)

1 der Wagen car → **des Wagens** of the car
 das Rauchen smoking → **des Rauchens** of smoking
 der Computer computer → **des Computers** of the computer
 der Reiter rider → **des Reiters** of the rider
2 der Sitz seat; residence → **des Sitzes** of the seat/residence
 der Arzt doctor → **des Arztes** of the doctor
 das Schloß castle → **des Schlosses** of the castle
3 das Kind →
 Die Zähne des Kindes waren faul geworden
 The child's teeth had decayed
 Der Name des Kinds war ihm unbekannt
 The child's name was not known to him
4 wegen seiner Krankheit because of his illness
 trotz ihrer Bemühungen despite her efforts
5 eines Tages one day
6 dem Wagen to the car
 der Frau to the woman
 dem Mädchen to the girl
7 zu welchem Zwecke? to what purpose?
8 nach Hause home
 sich zu Tode trinken/arbeiten
 to drink/work oneself to death
9 mit den Anwälten with the lawyers
 nach den Kindern after the children

10	SINGULAR	PLURAL
	das Auto	die Autos
	das Auto	die Autos
	des Autos	der Autos
	dem Auto	den Autos

11 Er gab dem Mann das Buch He gave the man the book
12 Sie half ihrer Mutter She helped her mother
13 Nach dem Essen ... After eating ...
14 Mir ist kalt I'm cold
15 Ich habe mir die Hände gewaschen I've washed my hands

The Formation of Plurals

The following pages show full noun declensions in all their
singular and plural forms.
Those nouns shown represent the most common types of
plural.

● Most feminine nouns add **-n**, **-en** or **-nen** to form their
plurals:

	singular	plural
nom	**die Frau**	**die Frauen**
acc	**die Frau**	**die Frauen**
gen	**der Frau**	**der Frauen**
dat	**der Frau**	**den Frauen**

● Many nouns have no plural ending.
These are mainly masculine or neuter nouns ending in **-en**,
-er, **-el**.
An umlaut is sometimes added to the vowel in the plural
forms.

	singular	plural
nom	**der Onkel**	**die Onkel**
acc	**den Onkel**	**die Onkel**
gen	**des Onkels**	**der Onkel**
dat	**dem Onkel**	**den Onkeln**

	singular	plural
nom	**der Apfel**	**die Äpfel**
acc	**den Apfel**	**die Äpfel**
gen	**des Apfels**	**der Äpfel**
dat	**dem Apfel**	**den Äpfeln**

Continued

The Formation of Plurals (ctd.)

- Many nouns form their plurals by adding ¨e

	singular	plural
nom	der Stuhl	die Stühle
acc	den Stuhl	die Stühle
gen	des Stuhl(e)s	der Stühle
dat	dem Stuhl(e)	den Stühlen

	singular	plural
nom	die Angst	die Ängste
acc	die Angst	die Ängste
gen	der Angst	der Ängste
dat	der Angst	den Ängsten

- Masculine and neuter nouns often add -e in the plural

	singular	plural
nom	das Schicksal	die Schicksale
acc	das Schicksal	die Schicksale
gen	des Schicksals	der Schicksale
dat	dem Schicksal(e)	den Schicksalen

- Masculine and neuter nouns sometimes add ¨er or -er

	singular	plural
nom	das Dach	die Dächer
acc	das Dach	die Dächer
gen	des Dach(e)s	der Dächer
dat	dem Dach(e)	den Dächern

Continued

The Formation of Plurals (ctd.)

Some Unusual Plurals

das Ministerium, die Ministerien Department(s)
das Prinzip, die Prinzipien principle(s)
das Thema, die Themen theme(s), topic(s), subject(s)
das Drama, die Dramen drama(s)
die Firma, die Firmen firm(s)
das Konto, die Konten bank account(s)
das Risiko, die Risiken risk(s)
das Komma, die Kommas or **Kommata** comma(s); decimal point(s)
das Baby, die Babys baby (babies)
der Klub, die Klubs club(s)
der Streik, die Streiks strike(s)
der Park, die Parks park(s)
der Chef, die Chefs boss(es), chief(s), head(s)
der Israeli, die Israelis Israeli(s)
das Restaurant, die Restaurants restaurant(s)
das Bonbon, die Bonbons sweet(s)
das Hotel, die Hotels hotel(s)
das Niveau, die Niveaus standard(s), level(s)

German singular/English plural nouns

Some nouns are always plural in English, but singular in German:

● Some of the most common examples are:

   eine Brille glasses, spectacles
   eine Schere scissors
   eine Hose trousers

● They are only used in the plural in German to mean more than one pair, e.g. **zwei Hosen** *two pairs of trousers*

The Declension of Nouns (ctd.)

"Weak" Masculine nouns

Some masculine nouns have a weak declension, which means that in all cases apart from the nominative singular, they end in **-en** or, if the word ends in a vowel, in **-n**

- The dictionary will often show such nouns as
  Junge *m* **-n, -n** boy
  Held *m* **-en, -en** hero

- Weak masculine nouns are declined as follows:

	singular	plural
nom	der Junge	die Jungen
acc	den Jungen	die Jungen
gen	des Jungen	der Jungen
dat	dem Jungen	den Jungen

- Masculine nouns falling into this category include:
  — those ending in **-og(e)** referring to males:
    der Psychologe, der Geologe, der Astrologe
  — those ending in **-aph** or **-oph**:
    der Paragraph, der Philosoph
  — those ending in **-nom** referring to males:
    der Astronom, der Gastronom
  — those ending in **-ant**:
    der Elefant, der Diamant
  — those ending in **-t** which refer to males:
    der Astronaut, der Komponist, der Architekt
  — miscellaneous others:
    der Chirurg, der Bauer, der Ochs, der Kollege, der Spatz, der Mensch, der Katholik, der Franzose

- **der Name** (*name*) has a different ending in the genitive singular, **-ns**: **des Namens**. Otherwise it is the same as **der Junge** shown above. Others in this category are: **der Buchstabe, der Glaube, der Gedanke, der Haufe, der Funke**.

The Declension of Proper Nouns

- Names of people and places add **-s** in the genitive singular unless they are preceded by the definite article or a demonstrative (→1)

- Where proper names end in a sibilant (**-s, -sch, -ß, -x, -z, -tz**) and this makes the genitive form with **-s** almost impossible to pronounce, they are best avoided altogether by using **von** followed by the dative case (→2)

- Personal names can be given diminutive forms if desired. These may be used as a sign of affection as well as with diminutive meaning (→3)

- **Herr** (*Mr.*) is always declined where it occurs as part of a proper name (→4)

- When articles or adjectives form part of a proper name (e.g. in the names of books, plays, hotels, restaurants *etc*), these are declined in the normal way (see pp.118 and 140) (→5)

- Surnames usually form their plurals by adding **-s**, unless they end in a sibilant, in which case they sometimes add **-ens**. They are often preceded by the definite article (→6)

Nouns of Measurement and Quantity

- These usually remain singular, even if preceded by a plural number (→7)

- The substance which they measure follows in the same case as the noun of quantity, and not in the genitive case as in English (→8)

1 **Peters Buch** Peter's book
  Klaras Mantel Clara's coat
  Die Werke Goethes Goethe's works
  BUT: **die Versenkung der Bismarck**
  the sinking of the Bismarck

2 **Das Buch von Hans** Hans' book
  Die Werke von Marx The works of Marx
  Die Freundin von Klaus Klaus's girlfriend

3 **von Deinem Sabinchen** from your Sabine
  Das kleine Peterchen hat uns dann ein Lied gesungen
  Then little Peter sang us a song

4 **an Herrn Schmidt** to Mr. Smith
  Sehr geehrte Herren Dear sirs

5 **im Weißen Schwan** in the White Swan
  Er hat "Den Zauberberg" schon gelesen
  He has already read "The Magic Mountain"
  nach Karl dem Großen after Charlemagne

6 **Die Schmidts haben uns eingeladen**
  The Smiths have invited us
  Die Zeißens haben uns eingeladen
  Mr. and Mrs. Zeiß have invited us

7 **Möchten Sie zwei Stück?**
  Would you like two?

8 **Er wollte zwei Kilo Kartoffeln**
  He wanted two kilos of potatoes
  Sie hat drei Tassen Kaffee getrunken
  She drank three cups of coffee
  Drei Glas Weißwein, bitte!
  Three glasses of white wine please

The Definite Article

In English the definite article *the* always keeps the same form
   the book/*the* books/with *the* books
In German, however, the definite article has many forms:

- In its singular form it changes for masculine, feminine and
  neuter nouns (→**1**)

- In its plural forms, it is the same for all genders (→**2**)

- The definite article is also used to show the function of the
  noun in the sentence by showing which case it is.
  There are four cases, as explained more fully on p.108:
    nominative for the subject or complement of the verb
    (→**3**)
    accusative for the object of the verb and after some
    prepositions (→**4**)
    genitive to show possession and after some prepositions
    (→**5**)
    dative for an indirect object (*to* or *for*) and after some
    prepositions and certain verbs (→**6**)

- The forms of the definite article are as follows:

		singular		plural
	masc	fem	neut	all genders
nom	**der**	**die**	**das**	**die**
acc	**den**	**die**	**das**	**die**
gen	**des**	**der**	**des**	**der**
dat	**dem**	**der**	**dem**	**den** (→**7**)

Continued

1 *masculine*:   **der Mann** the man
                    der Wagen the car
   feminine: **die Frau** the wife/woman
                die Blume the flower
   neuter: **das Ding** the thing
              das Mädchen the girl

2 **die Männer/die Frauen/die Dinge**
the men/the women/the things

3 **Der Mann ist jung** The man is young
Die Frau/das Kind ist jung The woman/the child is young

4 **Ich kenne den Mann/die Frau/das Kind**
I know the man/the woman/the child

5 **der Kopf des Mannes/der Frau/des Kindes**
the man's/woman's/child's head
Wegen des Mannes/der Frau/des Kindes
Because of the man/the woman/the child

6 **Ich gab es dem Mann/der Frau/dem Kind**
I gave it to the man/to the woman/to the child

7

		singular	
	masc	fem	neut
nom	**der Mann**	**die Frau**	**das Kind**
acc	**den Mann**	**die Frau**	**das Kind**
gen	**des Mann(e)s**	**der Frau**	**des Kind(e)s**
dat	**dem Mann(e)**	**der Frau**	**dem Kind(e)**

		plural	
	masc	fem	neut
nom	**die Männer**	**die Frauen**	**die Kinder**
acc	**die Männer**	**die Frauen**	**die Kinder**
gen	**der Männer**	**der Frauen**	**der Kinder**
dat	**den Männern**	**den Frauen**	**den Kindern**

Uses of the Definite Article

When to use and when not to use the definite article in German is one of the most difficult areas for the learner. The following guidelines show where German practice varies from English.

The definite article is used with:

- abstract and other nouns where something is being referred to as a whole or as a general idea (→**1**)
  Where these nouns are quantified or modified, the article is not used (→**2**)

- the genitive, unless the noun is a proper name or is acting as a proper name (→**3**)

- occasionally with proper names to make the sex or case clearer (→**4**)

- always with proper names preceded by an adjective (→**5**)

- sometimes with proper names in familiar contexts or for slight emphasis (→**6**)

- with masculine and feminine countries and districts (→**7**)

- with geographical names preceded by an adjective (→**8**)

- with names of seasons (→**9**)

- often with meals (→**10**)

- with the names of roads (→**11**)

Continued

1 Das Leben ist schön Life is wonderful

2 Es braucht Mut It needs (some) courage
 Gibt es dort Leben? Is there (any) life there?

3 Das Auto des Lehrers The teacher's car
 Peters Auto Peter's car
 Muttis Auto Mummy's car

4 Er hat es Frau Lehmann gegeben
 Er hat es der Frau Lehmann gegeben
 He gave it to Frau Lehmann

5 Der alte Herr Brockhaus ist damals sehr taub gewesen
 Old Mr. Brockhaus went very deaf at that time

6 Ich habe heute den Peter gesehen
 I saw Peter today
 Du hast es aber nicht der Petra geschenkt!
 You haven't given it to *Petra*!

7 Deutschland ist sehr schön Germany is very beautiful
 Die Schweiz ist auch schön Switzerland is also lovely

8 Im (= in dem) **heutigen Deutschland**
 In today's Germany

9 Im (= in dem) **Sommer gehen wir schwimmen**
 We go swimming in summer
 Der Winter kommt bald
 Soon it will be winter

10 Das Abendessen wird ab acht Uhr serviert
 Dinner is served from eight o'clock
 Was gibt's zum (= zu dem) **Mittagessen?**
 What's for lunch?
 BUT
 Um 8 Uhr ist Frühstück
 Breakfast is at 8 o'clock

11 Sie wohnt jetzt in der Geisenerstraße
 She lives in Geisener Road now

Uses of the Definite Article (ctd.)

- with months of the year except after **seit/nach/vor** (→1)

- instead of the possessive adjective to refer to parts of the body and items of clothing (→2)
  A reflexive pronoun or noun in the dative case is used if it is necessary to clarify to whom the parts of the body belong (→3)

- in expressions of price, to mean *each/per/a* (→4)

- with certain common expressions (→5)

Other Uses

- The definite article can be used with demonstrative meaning (→6)

- After certain prepositions, forms of the definite article can be shortened (see p.198 ff).
  Some of these forms are best used in informal situations (→7)
  Others are commonly and correctly used in formal contexts (→8, 1, 5)

The definite article may be omitted in German:

- in certain set expressions (→9)

- in *preposition* + *adjective* + *noun* combinations (→10)
  For the declension of adjectives without the article see p.142.

1 Wir fahren im (= in dem) September weg
We are going away in September
Wir sind seit September hier
We have been here since September

2 Er legte den Hut auf den Tisch
He laid his hat on the table
Ich drücke die Daumen I'm keeping my fingers crossed

3 Er hat sich die Hände schon gewaschen
He has already washed his hands
Er hat dem Kind schon die Hände gewaschen
He has already washed the child's hands

4 Die kosten ...   They cost ...
... fünf Mark das Pfund   ... five marks a pound
... sechs Mark das Stück   ... six marks each

5 in die Stadt fahren to go into town
zur (= zu der) Schule gehen to go to school
mit der Post by post
mit dem Zug/Bus/Auto by train/bus/car
im (= in dem) Gefängnis in prison

6 Du willst das Buch lesen!
You want to read *that* book!

7 für das → fürs; vor dem → vorm; um das → ums *etc*

8 an dem → am; zu dem → zum; zu der → zur *etc*

9 von Beruf by profession
nach Wunsch as desired
mit Kind und Kegel with bag and baggage
Nachrichten hören to listen to the news

10 Mit gebeugtem Rücken, ...   Bending his back, ...

The Indefinite Article

Like the definite article, the form of the indefinite article varies depending on the gender and case of the noun (→**1**) It has no plural forms (→**2**)

The indefinite article is declined as follows:

	masc	fem	neut	
nom	**ein**	**eine**	**ein**	
acc	**einen**	**eine**	**ein**	
gen	**eines**	**einer**	**eines**	
dat	**einem**	**einer**	**einem**	(→**3**)

● The indefinite article is omitted in the following:

— descriptions of people by profession, religion, nationality etc (→**4**)
But note that the article is included when an adjective precedes the noun (→**5**)

— in certain fixed expressions (→**6**)

— after **als** *as a* (→**7**)

Continued

1 **Da ist ein Auto** There's a car
   Er hat eine Wohnung He has a flat
   Sie gab es einem Kind She gave it to a child

2 **Autos sind in letzter Zeit teurer geworden**
   Cars have become more expensive recently

3

	MASC	SINGULAR FEM	NEUT
NOM	**ein Mann**	**eine Frau**	**ein Kind**
ACC	**einen Mann**	**eine Frau**	**ein Kind**
GEN	**eines Mann(e)s**	**einer Frau**	**eines Kind(e)s**
DAT	**einem Mann(e)**	**einer Frau**	**einem Kind(e)**

4 **Sie ist Kinderärztin** She's a paediatrician
   Sie ist Deutsche She's (a) German

5 **Sie ist eine sehr geschickte Kinderärztin**
   She's a very clever paediatrician

6 **Es ist Geschmackssache** It's a question of taste
   Tatsache ist ...   It's a fact ...
   Ich habe Kopfschmerzen I've got a headache

7 **Als Ausländer ist er hier nicht wahlberechtigt**
   As a foreigner he doesn't have the vote here
   ... und ich rede nun als Vater von vier Kindern
   ... and I'm talking now as a father of four

The Indefinite Article (ctd.)

In German, a separate negative form of the indefinite article exists.
It is declined exactly like **ein** in the singular and also has plural forms:

	masc	singular fem	neut	plural all genders
nom	**kein**	**keine**	**kein**	**keine**
acc	**keinen**	**keine**	**kein**	**keine**
gen	**keines**	**keiner**	**keines**	**keiner**
dat	**keinem**	**keiner**	**keinem**	**keinen** (→1)

● It has the meanings *no/not a/not one/not any* (→2)

● It is used even where the equivalent *positive* phrase has no article (→3)

● It is also used in many idiomatic expressions (→4)

● **nicht ein** may be used instead of **kein** where the **ein** is to be emphasized (→5)

1

| | SINGULAR | |
MASC	FEM	NEUT
NOM **kein Mann**	**keine Frau**	**kein Kind**
ACC **keinen Mann**	**keine Frau**	**kein Kind**
GEN **keines Mann(e)s**	**keiner Frau**	**keines Kind(e)s**
DAT **keinem Mann (e)**	**keiner Frau**	**keinem Kind(e)**

PLURAL		
NOM **keine Männer**	**keine Frauen**	**keine Kinder**
ACC **keine Männer**	**keine Frauen**	**keine Kinder**
GEN **keiner Männer**	**keiner Frauen**	**keiner Kinder**
DAT **keinen Männern**	**keinen Frauen**	**keinen Kindern**

2 **Er hatte keine Geschwister**
He had no brothers or sisters
Ich sehe keinen Unterschied I don't see any difference
Das ist keine richtige Antwort That's no answer
Kein Mensch hat es gesehen Not one person has seen it

3 **Er hatte Angst davor** He was frightened
Er hatte keine Angst davor He wasn't frightened

4 **Er hatte kein Geld mehr** All his money was gone
Es waren keine drei Monate vorbeigegangen, als ...
It was less than three months later that ...
Es hat mich keine zehn Mark gekostet
It cost me less than ten marks

5 **Nicht ein Kind hat es singen können**
Not *one* child could sing it

Words declined like the Definite Article

The following have endings similar to those of the definite article shown on p.118:

> **jeder, jede, jedes** each, each one, every
> **jener, jene, jenes** that, that one, those
> **dieser, diese, dieses** this, this one, these
> **solcher, solche, solches** such/such a
> **sämtliche** all, entire (*usually plural*)
> **mancher, manche, manches** many a/some
> **einiger, einige, einiges** some, a few, a little
> **welcher, welche, welches** which, which one
> **aller, alle, alles** all, all of them
> **irgendwelcher, -e, -es** some or other
> **beide** both (*plural only*)

● These words can be used as: articles (→**1**)
  pronouns (→**2**)

● They have the following endings:

| | singular | | | plural |
	masc	fem	neut	all genders
nom	-er	-e	-es	-e
acc	-en	-e	-es	-e
gen	-es/-en	-er	-es/-en	-er
dat	-em	-er	-em	-en

Example declensions are shown on p.134ff.

● **einiger** and **irgendwelcher** use the **-en** genitive ending before masculine or neuter nouns ending in **-s** (→**3**)
jeder, welcher, mancher and **solcher** may also do so (→**4**)

Continued

1 Dieser Mann kommt aus Südamerika
   This man comes from South America
   Er geht jeden Tag ins Büro
   He goes to the office every day
   Manche Leute können das nicht
   A good many people can't do it

2 Willst du diesen? Do you want this one?
   In manchem hat er recht He's right about some things
   Man kann ja nicht alles wissen
   You can't know everything
   Es gibt manche, die keinen Alkohol mögen
   There are some people who don't like alcohol

3 wegen irgendwelchen Streites
   on account of some argument or other

4 der Besitz solchen Reichtums
   the possession of such wealth
   trotz jeden Versuchs
   despite all attempts

Words declined like the Definite Article

(ctd.)

- Adjectives following these words have the weak declension (see p.140) (→1)
  Exceptions are the plural forms of **einige**, which are followed by the strong declension (see p.142) (→2)

Further points

- **solcher, beide, sämtliche** may be used after another article or possessive adjective. They then take weak (see p.140) or mixed (see p.142) adjectival endings, as appropriate (→3)

- Although **beide** generally has plural forms only, one singular form does exist. This is in the neuter nominative and accusative: **beides** (→4)

- **dies** often replaces the nominative and accusative **dieses** and **diese** when used as a pronoun (→5)

- **alles** as the genitive singular of the pronoun **aller** is used with the demonstrative **das** (→6)

- A fixed form **all** exists which is used together with other articles or possessive pronouns (→7)

- **ganz** can also be used to replace both the inflected form **aller/alle/alles** and the uninflected **all das/dieses/sein** etc.
  It is declined as a normal adjective (see p. 140) (→8)
  It must be used with collective nouns, in time phrases and geographical references (→9)

Continued

1   **dieses alte Auto** this old car
     aus irgendwelchem dummen Grunde
     for some stupid reason or other
     welche neuen Waren? which new goods?

2   **Die sind einige gute Freunde von mir**
     These are some good friends of mine

3   **Ein solches Kleid habe ich früher auch getragen**
     I used to wear a dress like that too
     Diese beiden Männer haben es gesehen
     Both of these men have seen it

4   **Beides ist richtig** Both are right
     Sie hat beides genommen She took both

5   **Hast du dies schon gelesen?**
     Have you already read this?
     Dies sind meine neuen Sachen
     These are my new things

6   **Der Besitzer alles, das wir gerade besichtigt hatten ...**
     The owner of everything that we had just looked at ...

7   **All sein Mut war verschwunden**
     All his courage had vanished
     mit all diesem Geld   with all this money

8   **mit dem ganzen Geld** with all this money

9   **die ganze Gesellschaft** the entire company
     Es hat den ganzen Tag geschneit
     It snowed the whole day long
     Im ganzen Land gab es kein besseres
     There wasn't a better one in the whole country

Words declined like the Definite Article
(ctd.)

- **derjenige/diejenige/dasjenige** (*the one, those*) is declined exactly as the definite article plus an adjective in the weak declension (see p.140) (→1)

- **derselbe/dieselbe/dasselbe** (*the same, the same one*) is declined in the same way as **derjenige** (→2)

  After prepositions however, the normal contracted forms of the definite article are used for the appropriate parts of **derselbe** (→3)

Continued

1

	SINGULAR	
MASC	FEM	NEUT
derjenige Mann	diejenige Frau	dasjenige Kind
denjenigen Mann	diejenige Frau	dasjenige Kind
desjenigen Mann(e)s	derjenigen Frau	desjenigen Kind(e)s
demjenigen Mann(e)	derjenigen Frau	demjenigen Kind(e)

	PLURAL	
MASC	FEM	NEUT
diejenigen Männer	diejenigen Frauen	diejenigen Kinder
diejenigen Männer	diejenigen Frauen	diejenigen Kinder
derjenigen Männer	derjenigen Frauen	derjenigen Kinder
denjenigen Männern	denjenigen Frauen	denjenigen Kindern

2

	SINGULAR	
MASC	FEM	NEUT
derselbe Mann	dieselbe Frau	dasselbe Kind
denselben Mann	dieselbe Frau	dasselbe Kind
desselben Mann(e)s	derselben Frau	desselben Kind(e)s
demselben Mann(e)	derselben Frau	demselben Kind(e)

	PLURAL	
MASC	FEM	NEUT
dieselben Männer	dieselben Frauen	dieselben Kinder
dieselben Männer	dieselben Frauen	dieselben Kinder
derselben Männer	derselben Frauen	derselben Kinder
denselben Männern	denselben Frauen	denselben Kindern

3 zur selben (= zu derselben) **Zeit** at the same time
im selben (= in demselben) **Zimmer** in the same room

Words declined like the Definite Article
(ctd.)

Sample Declensions in full

dieser, diese, dieses this, this one

	MASC	FEM	NEUT
		SINGULAR	
nom	**dieser Mann**	diese Frau	dieses Kind
acc	**diesen Mann**	diese Frau	dieses Kind
gen	**dieses Mann(e)s**	dieser Frau	dieses Kind(e)s
dat	**diesem Mann(e)**	dieser Frau	diesem Kind(e)

	MASC	FEM	NEUT
		PLURAL	
nom	**diese Männer**	diese Frauen	diese Kinder
acc	**diese Männer**	diese Frauen	diese Kinder
gen	**dieser Männer**	dieser Frauen	dieser Kinder
dat	**diesen Männern**	diesen Frauen	diesen Kindern

jener, jene, jenes that, that one

	MASC	FEM	NEUT
		SINGULAR	
nom	**jener Mann**	jene Frau	jenes Kind
acc	**jenen Mann**	jene Frau	jenes Kind
gen	**jenes Mann(e)s**	jener Frau	jenes Kind(e)s
dat	**jenem Mann(e)**	jener Frau	jenem Kind(e)

	MASC	FEM	NEUT
		PLURAL	
nom	**jene Männer**	jene Frauen	jene Kinder
acc	**jene Männer**	jene Frauen	jene Kinder
gen	**jener Männer**	jener Frauen	jener Kinder
dat	**jenen Männern**	jenen Frauen	jenen Kindern

jeder, jede, jedes each, every, everybody

	SINGULAR		
	MASC	FEM	NEUT
nom	jeder Wagen	jede Minute	jedes Bild
acc	jeden Wagen	jede Minute	jedes Bild
gen	jedes Wagens	jeder Minute	jedes Bild(e)s
	(jeden Wagens)		(jeden Bild(e)s)
dat	jedem Wagen	jeder Minute	jedem Bild(e)

welcher, welche, welches which?, which

	SINGULAR		
	MASC	FEM	NEUT
nom	welcher Preis	welche Sorte	welches Mädchen
acc	welchen Preis	welche Sorte	welches Mädchen
gen	welches Preises	welcher Sorte	welches Mädchens
	(welchen Preises)		(welchen Mädchens)
dat	welchem Preis	welcher Sorte	welchem Mädchen

	PLURAL		
	MASC	FEM	NEUT
nom	welche Preise	welche Sorten	welche Mädchen
acc	welche Preise	welche Sorten	welche Mädchen
gen	welcher Preise	welcher Sorten	welcher Mädchen
dat	welchen Preisen	welchen Sorten	welchen Mädchen

Words declined like the Indefinite Article

The following have the same declension pattern as the indefinite articles **ein** and **kein** (see pp.124 and 126):

The possessive adjectives

mein my (→**1**)
dein your (*singular familiar*)
sein his/its
ihr her/its (→**2**)
unser our
euer your (*plural familiar*)
ihr their (→**2**)
Ihr your (*polite singular and plural*)

These words are declined as follows:

| | singular | | | plural |
	masc	fem	neut	all genders
nom	—	-e	—	-e
acc	-en	-e	—	-e
gen	-es	-er	-es	-er
dat	-em	-er	-em	-en

- Adjectives following these determiners have the mixed declension forms (see p.142), e.g.:

    sein altes Auto his old car

- **irgendein** *some ... or other* also follows this declension pattern in the singular.
  Its plural form is **irgendwelche** (see p.128).

1 mein, meine, mein my

SINGULAR

	MASC	FEM	NEUT
nom	mein Bruder	meine Schwester	mein Kind
acc	meinen Bruder	meine Schwester	mein Kind
gen	meines Bruders	meiner Schwester	meines Kind(e)s
dat	meinem Bruder	meiner Schwester	meinem Kind(e)

PLURAL

	MASC	FEM	NEUT
nom	meine Brüder	meine Schwestern	meine Kinder
acc	meine Brüder	meine Schwestern	meine Kinder
gen	meiner Brüder	meiner Schwestern	meiner Kinder
dat	meinen Brüdern	meinen Schwestern	meinen Kindern

2 ihr, ihre, ihr her/its/their

SINGULAR

	MASC	FEM	NEUT
nom	ihr Bruder	ihre Schwester	ihr Kind
acc	ihren Bruder	ihre Schwester	ihr Kind
gen	ihres Bruders	ihrer Schwester	ihres Kind(e)s
dat	ihrem Bruder	ihrer Schwester	ihrem Kind(e)

PLURAL

	MASC	FEM	NEUT
nom	ihre Brüder	ihre Schwestern	ihre Kinder
acc	ihre Brüder	ihre Schwestern	ihre Kinder
gen	ihrer Brüder	ihrer Schwestern	ihrer Kinder
dat	ihren Brüdern	ihren Schwestern	ihren Kindern

Indefinite Adjectives

These are adjectives used in place of, or together with, an article:

mehrere (*plural only*) several
viel much, a lot, many
wenig little, a little, few
ander other, different

- After the definite article and words declined like it (see p.128) these adjectives have weak declension endings (→1)
  Adjectives following the indefinite adjectives are also weak (→2)

- After **ein, kein, irgendein** or the possessive adjectives, they have mixed declension endings (→3)
  Adjectives following the indefinite adjectives are also mixed in declension (→4)

- When used without a preceding article, **ander** and **mehrere** have strong declension endings (→5)

- When used without a preceding article, **viel** and **wenig** may be declined as follows, though in the singular they are usually undeclined (→6):

| | singular | | | plural |
	masc	fem	neut	all genders
nom	viel	viel	viel	viele
acc	viel	viel	viel	viele
gen	vielen	vieler	vielen	vieler
dat	viel(em)	vieler	viel(em)	vielen

- Any adjective following **viel** or **wenig** has strong endings (→7)

1 Die wenigen Kuchen, die übriggeblieben waren ...
The few cakes which were left over ...

2 Die vielen interessanten Ideen, die ans Licht kamen
The many interesting ideas which came to light

3 Ihr anderes Auto ist in der Werkstatt
Their other car is in for repair

4 Mehrere gute Freunde waren gekommen
Several good friends had come

5 Mehrere gute Freunde waren gekommen
Several good friends had come

Er war anderer Meinung
He was of a different opinion

6 Es wurde viel Bier getrunken
They drank a lot of beer

Sie essen nur wenig Obst
They don't eat a lot of fruit

7 Er kaufte viele billige Sachen
He bought a lot of cheap things

Es wurde viel gutes Bier getrunken
They drank a lot of good beer

Sie essen wenig importiertes Obst
They don't eat a lot of imported fruit

The Declension of Adjectives

There are two ways of using adjectives.

- They can be used **attributively**, where the adjective comes before the noun: *the new book*

- They can be used **non-attributively**, where the adjective comes after the verb: *the book is new*

- In English the adjective does not change its form no matter how it is used.
  In German, however, adjectives remain unchanged only when used the second way (non-attributively) (→**1**)
  Used attributively, adjectives change to show the number, gender and case of the noun they precede (→**2**)
  The endings also depend on the nature of the article which precedes them (→**3**)

There are three sets of endings:

1 The weak declension

These are the endings used after **der** and those words declined like it as shown on p.128 (→**4**)

	singular			plural
	masc	fem	neut	all genders
nom	-e	-e	-e	-en
acc	-en	-e	-e	-en
gen	-en	-en	-en	-en
dat	-en	-en	-en	-en

Continued

1 **Das Buch ist neu** The book is new
Der Vortrag war sehr langweilig
The lecture was very boring

2 **Das neue Buch ist da** The new book has arrived
**Während des langweiligen Vortrags sind wir alle
eingeschlafen**
We all fell asleep during the boring lecture

3 **der junge Rechtsanwalt** the young lawyer
ein junger Rechtsanwalt a young lawyer
manch junger Rechtsanwalt many a young lawyer

4

SINGULAR

	MASC	FEM	NEUT
nom	**der alte Mann**	**die alte Frau**	**das alte Haus**
acc	**den alten Mann**	**die alte Frau**	**das alte Haus**
gen	**des alten Mann(e)s**	**der alten Frau**	**des alten Hauses**
dat	**dem alten Mann(e)**	**der alten Frau**	**dem alten Haus(e)**

PLURAL

	MASC	FEM	NEUT
nom	**die alten Männer**	**die alten Frauen**	**die alten Häuser**
acc	**die alten Männer**	**die alten Frauen**	**die alten Häuser**
gen	**der alten Männer**	**der alten Frauen**	**der alten Häuser**
dat	**den alten Männern**	**den alten Frauen**	**den alten Häusern**

The Declension of Adjectives (ctd.)

2 The mixed declension

These are the endings used after **ein, kein, irgendein** and the possessive adjectives (see p.136) (→1):

	singular			plural
	masc	fem	neut	all genders
nom	-er	-e	-es	-en
acc	-en	-e	-es	-en
gen	-en	-en	-en	-en
dat	-en	-en	-en	-en (→2)

3 The strong declension

Strong declension endings:

	singular			plural
	masc	fem	neut	all genders
nom	-er	-e	-es	-e
acc	-en	-e	-es	-e
gen	-en	-er	-en	-er
dat	-em	-er	-em	-en (→3)

These endings are used where there is no preceding article. The article is omitted more frequently in German than in English, especially in combinations "preposition + adjective + noun" (see p.122).

These endings enable the adjective to do the work of the missing article by showing case, number and gender (→4)

Continued

1 Meine neue Stelle ist bei einer großen Druckerei
My new job is with a large printing works
Ihre frühere Theorie ist jetzt bestätigt worden
Her earlier theory has now been proved true

2

SINGULAR

MASC	FEM	NEUT
ein langer Weg	eine lange Reise	ein langes Spiel
einen langen Weg	eine lange Reise	ein langes Spiel
eines langen Wegs	einer langen Reise	eines langen Spieles
einem langen Weg	einer langen Reise	einem langen Spiel

PLURAL

ALL GENDERS

nom	ihre langen Wege / Reisen / Spiele
acc	ihre langen Wege / Reisen / Spiele
gen	ihrer langen Wege / Reisen / Spiele
dat	ihren langen Wegen / Reisen / Spielen

3

SINGULAR

	MASC	FEM	NEUT
nom	guter Käse	gute Marmelade	gutes Bier
acc	guten Käse	gute Marmelade	gutes Bier
gen	guten Käses	guter Marmelade	guten Biers
dat	gutem Käse	guter Marmelade	gutem Bier

PLURAL

ALL GENDERS

nom	gute Käse / Marmeladen / Biere
acc	gute Käse / Marmeladen / Biere
gen	guter Käse / Marmeladen / Biere
dat	guten Käsen / Marmeladen / Bieren

4 nach kurzer Fahrt after a short journey
   mit gleichem Gehalt with the same salary

The Declension of Adjectives (ctd.)

- Strong declension endings are also used after any of the following where they are not preceded by an article or other determiner:

  ein bißchen a little, a bit of
  ein wenig a little
  ein paar a few, a couple (→1)
  weniger fewer, less
  einige (*plural forms only*) some
  allerlei/allerhand all kinds of, all sorts of
  keinerlei no ... whatsoever, no ... at all
  mancherlei various, a number of
  etwas some, any (*singular*) (→2)
  mehr more
  lauter nothing but, sheer, pure
  solch such
  vielerlei various, all sorts of, many different
  mehrerlei several kinds of
  was für what, what kind of
  (*note that* **was für ein** *takes the mixed declension*)
  welcherlei what kind of, what sort of
  viel much, many, a lot of
  wievielerlei how many kinds of
  welch! what! what a! (→3)
  manch many a
  wenig little, few, not much (→4)
  zweierlei/dreierlei *etc* two/three *etc* kinds of
  zwei, drei *etc* two, three *etc* (→5)
  (*but note that the mixed declension is used after* **ein**)

- The strong declension is also required after possessives where no other word indicates the case, gender and number (→6)

Continued

1 **ein paar gute Tips** (*strong declension*)
a couple of good tips

2 **Etwas starken Pfeffer zugeben** (*strong*)
Add a little strong pepper

3 **Welch herrliches Wetter!** (*strong*)
What splendid weather!

4 **Es gab damals nur wenig frisches Obst** (*strong*)
At that time there was little fresh fruit
BUT
Das wenige frische Obst, das es damals gab ... (*weak*)
The little fresh fruit that was then available ...

5 **Zwei große Jungen waren herangekommen** (*strong*)
Two big boys had come along
BUT
Die zwei großen Jungen, die herangekommen waren (*weak*)
The two big boys who had come along
Meine zwei großen Jungen (*mixed*)
My two big sons

6 **Peters altes Buch** (*strong*)
Peter's old book

Muttis neues Auto (*strong*)
Mum's new car

The Declension of Adjectives (ctd.)

Some spelling changes when adjectives are declined

- When the adjective **hoch** (*high*) is declined, its stem changes to **hoh-** (→1)

- Adjectives ending in **-el** lose the **-e-** of their stem when inflected, i.e. when endings are added (→2)

- Adjectives with an **-er** ending often lose the **-e-** from the ending when inflected (→3)

The participles as adjectives

- The present participle can be used as an adjective with normal adjectival endings (pp.140 to 143) (→4)
  The present participles of **sein** and **haben** cannot be used in this way

- The past participle can also be used as an adjective in this way (→5)

Adjectives followed by the dative case

A *dative case* is required after many adjectives e.g. (→6):
ähnlich similar to
bekannt familiar to
dankbar grateful to
fremd alien to
gleich all the same to; like
leicht easy for
nah close to
peinlich painful for
unbekannt unknown to

1 **Das Gebäude ist hoch** The building is high
   BUT
   ein hohes Gebäude a high building

2 **Das Zimmer ist dunkel** The room is dark
   BUT
   in dem dunklen Zimmer in the dark room

3 **Das Auto war teuer** The car was expensive
   BUT
   Er kaufte ein teures Auto He bought an expensive car

4 **die werdende Mutter** the mother-to-be
   ein lachendes Kind a laughing child

5 **meine verlorenen Sachen** my lost things
   die ausgebeuteten Arbeiter
   the exploited workers

6 **Ist dir das bekannt?** Do you know about it?
   Ich wäre Ihnen dankbar, wenn ...
   I should be grateful to you if ...
   Diese Sache ist mir etwas peinlich
   This matter is somewhat embarrassing for me
   Solche Gedanken waren ihm fremd
   Such thoughts were alien to him

Adjectives used as nouns

All adjectives in German, and those participles used as adjectives, can also be used as nouns. These are often called **adjectival nouns**.

- Adjectives and participles used as nouns have:
  a capital letter like other nouns   (→1)
  declension endings like other adjectives, depending on the preceding article, if any (see below) (→2)

Declension endings for adjectives used as nouns:

- after **der, dieser** and words like it shown on p.128, the normal *weak* adjective endings apply (see p.140) (→3)
  Der Junge (*the boy*) is an exception and is declined like a weak masculine noun, as shown on p.115.

- after **ein, kein, irgendein** and the possessive adjectives shown on p.136, the *mixed* adjective endings apply (see p.142) (→4)

- where no article is present, or after those words shown on p.144, the *strong* adjective endings are used (see p.142) (→5)
  When another adjective precedes the adjectival noun, the *strong* endings become *weak* in two instances:

    in the *dative singular* (→6)

    in the *nominative and accusative plural* after a possessive, where the strong endings might cause confusion with the singular feminine form (→7)

- Some adjectival nouns have become part of set expressions, and these tend to be written without the capital letter (→8)

1 **der Angestellte** the employee

2 **die Angestellte** the female employee
 das Neue daran ist ... the new thing about it is ...

3 **für den Angeklagten** for the accused
 mit dieser Bekannten with this (*female*) friend

4 **Kein Angestellter darf hier rauchen**
 No employee may smoke here
 Sie machten einen Ausflug mit ihren Bekannten zusammen
 They went on a trip with their friends

5 **Etwas Besonderes ist geschehen**
 Something special has happened

6 **Ich hatte es Peters jüngerem Verwandten versprochen**
 I had promised it to Peter's young relative

7 **Peters jüngere Verwandten wollten es haben**
 Peter's young relatives wanted to have it

8 **Es bleibt beim alten** Things remain as they were
 Er hat den ersten besten genommen
 He took the first that came to hand

Miscellaneous points

Adjectives of nationality

- These are not spelt with a capital letter in German except in public or official names (→**1**)

- However, when used as a noun to refer to the language, a capital is used (→**2**)

- In German, for expressions like *he is English/he is German* etc a noun or adjectival noun is used instead of an adjective (→**3**)

Adjectives derived from place names

- These are formed by adding **-er** to names of towns (→**4**)

- They are never inflected (→**5**)

- Adjectives from **die Schweiz** and from certain regions can also be formed in this way (→**6**)

- Such adjectives may be used as nouns denoting the inhabitants of a town.
  They are then declined as normal nouns (see p.98ff) (→**7**)
  The feminine form is made by adding **-in** in the singular and **-innen** in the plural (→**8**)

- Certain names ending in **-en** drop the **-e-** or the **-en** of their ending before adding **-er** (→**9**)

- A second type of adjective formed from place names exists, ending in **-isch** and spelt with a small letter. It is inflected as a normal adjective (see p.140).
  It is used mainly where the speaker is referring to the mood of, or something typical of that place (→**10**)

1 **Die deutsche Sprache** the German language
  Das französische Volk The French people
  BUT **Die Deutsche Schlaf- und Speisewagen Gesellschaft**

2 **Sie sprechen kein Englisch** They don't speak English

3 **Er ist Deutscher** He is German
  Sie ist Deutsche She is German

4 **Kölner, Frankfurter, Düsseldorfer** *etc*

5 **der Kölner Dom** Cologne cathedral
  ein Frankfurter Würstchen a frankfurter sausage

6 **Schweizer Käse** Swiss cheese

7 **Die Sprache des Kölners heißt Kölsch**
  Von den Frankfurtern ...

8 **Die Kölnerin, die Kölnerinnen**
  Die Londonerin, die Londonerinnen

9 **München → der Münchner**
  Bremen → der Bremer
  Göttingen → der Göttinger

10 **Ein richtig frankfurterischer Ausdruck**
   A real Frankfurt expression
   Er spricht etwas münchnerisch
   He has something of a Munich accent

The Comparison of Adjectives

Adjectives have three basic forms of comparison:

A simple form used to describe something or someone:

e.g. a *little* house/the house is *little*

- This form is fully dealt with on pp. 140 to 147.

- Simple forms are used in *as ... as | not as ... as* comparisons (→**1**)

A comparative form used to compare two things or persons:

e.g. he is *bigger* than his brother

- In German, comparatives are formed by adding **-er** to the simple form (→**2**)

- *than* in comparative statements is translated by **als** (→**3**)

- Unlike English, the vast majority of German adjectives, including those of several syllables, form their comparatives in this way (→**4**)

- Many adjectives modify the stem vowel when forming their comparatives, as in the common examples shown opposite (→**5**)

Continued

1 so ... wie as ... as:
  Er ist so gut wie sein Bruder
  He is as good as his brother

  ebenso ... wie just as ... as:
  Er war ebenso glücklich wie ich
  He was just as happy as I was

  zwei/dreimal *etc* **so ... wie**
  twice/three *etc* times as ... as:
  Er war zweimal so grouder
  He was twice as big as his brother

  nicht so ... wie not as ... as:
  Er ist nicht so alt wie du
  He is not as old as you

2 klein / kleiner small / smaller
  schön / schöner lovely / lovelier

3 Er ist kleiner als seine Schwester
  He is smaller than his sister

4 bequem / bequemer comfortable / more comfortable
  gebildet / gebildeter educated / more educated
  effektiv / effektiver effective / more effective

5 alt / älter old / older
  stark / stärker strong / stronger
  schwach / schwächer weak / weaker
  scharf / schärfer sharp / sharper
  lang / länger long / longer
  kurz / kürzer short / shorter
  warm / wärmer warm / warmer
  kalt / kälter cold / colder
  hart / härter hard / harder
  groß / gröber big / bigger

Comparison of Adjectives (ctd.)

- Adjectives whose simple form ends in **-el** lose the **-e-** before adding the comparative ending **-er** (→**1**)

- Adjectives with a diphthong followed by **-er** in their simple forms also drop the **-e-** before adding **-er** (→**2**)

- Adjectives whose simple form ends in **-en** or **-er** may drop the **-e-** of the simple form when adjectival endings are added to their comparative forms (→**3**)

- With a few adjectives, comparative forms may be used not only for comparison, but also to render the idea of "-ish" or "rather ..."
  Some common examples are:

älter elderly	**dünner** thinnish
größer largish	**kürzer** shortish
kleiner smallish	**jünger** youngish
dicker fattish	**neuer** newish (→**4**)

- When used attributively (*before* the noun), comparative forms are declined in exactly the same way as simple adjectives (see pp.140 to 147) (→**4, 5**)

A superlative form used to compare three or more persons or things:

  e.g. he is *the biggest/the best*

- Superlatives are formed by adding **-st** to the simple adjective. The vowel is modified, as for comparative forms, where applicable.
  Superlative forms are generally used with an article and take endings accordingly (see p. 140) (→**6**)

Continued

1 **eitel / eitler** vain / vainer
    dunkel / dünkler dark / darker

2 **sauer / saurer** sour / more sour
    die saurere Zitrone the sourer lemon
    Der Wein ist saurer geworden
    The wine has grown more sour
    teuer / teurer expensive / more expensive
    Das ist eine teurere Sorte
    That is a more expensive kind
    Die Neuen sind teurer
    The new ones are more expensive

3 **finster / finsterer** dark / darker
    ein finstreres Gesicht
    OR
    ein finstereres Gesicht
    a grimmer face

4 **ein älterer Herr** an elderly gentleman
    die dickere Dame the stoutish lady
    Ich werde mir ein Neueres kaufen
    I shall buy myself a newish one

5 **Die jüngere Schwester ist größer als die ältere**
    The younger sister is bigger than the older
    Mein kleinerer Bruder geht jetzt zur Schule
    My younger brother goes to school now

6 **Er ist der Älteste** He is the oldest
    Ihr erfolgreichster Versuch war im Herbst 1980
    Her most successful attempt was in the autumn of 1980

Comparison of Adjectives (ctd.)

● Many adjectives form their superlative forms by adding **-est** instead of **-st** where pronunciation would otherwise be difficult or unaesthetic (→1)

● The English superlative *most* meaning *very* can be shown in German by any of the following (→2):

äußerst
sehr
besonders
außerordentlich
höchst (not with monosyllabic words)
furchtbar (conversational only)
richtig (conversational only)

Some irregular comparative and superlative forms

SIMPLE FORM	COMPARATIVE	SUPERLATIVE
gut	**besser**	**der beste**
hoch	**höher**	**der höchste**
viel	**mehr**	**der meiste**
nah	**näher**	**der nächste**

1 **der/die/das schlechteste** the worst
  der/die/das schmerzhafteste the most painful
  der/die/das süßeste the sweetest
  der/die/das neueste the newest
  der/die/das stolzeste the proudest
  der/die/das frischeste the freshest

2 **Er ist ein äußerst begabter Mensch**
  He is a most gifted person

  Das Essen war besonders schlecht
  The food was really/most dreadful

  Der Wein war furchtbar teuer!
  The wine was dreadfully/most expensive!

  Das sieht richtig komisch aus
  That looks really/most funny

Personal Pronouns

As in English, personal pronouns change their form depending on their function in the sentence:
  I saw him | He saw me | We saw her (→1)

The personal pronouns are declined as follows (→2):

NOMINATIVE	ACCUSATIVE	DATIVE
ich I	**mich** me	**mir** to/for me
du you	**dich** you	**dir** to/for you
er he/it	**ihn** him/it	**ihm** to/for him/it
sie she/it	**sie** her/it	**ihr** to/for her/it
es it/he/she	**es** it/him/her	**ihm** to/for it/him/her
wir we	**uns** us	**uns** to/for us
ihr you (*plural*)	**euch** you	**euch** to/for you
sie they	**sie** them	**ihnen** to/for them
Sie you (*polite*)	**Sie** you	**Ihnen** to/for you
man one	**einen** one	**einem** to/for one

- As can be seen from the above table, there are three ways of addressing people in German, by **du, ihr** or **Sie**.
  All three forms are illustrated overleaf.

- Personal pronouns in the dative require no preposition when acting as indirect object, i.e. *to* me, *to* him *etc* (→3)

Continued

1 Ich sah ihn I saw him
Er sah mich He saw me
Wir sahen sie We saw her

2 Wir sind mit ihnen spazierengegangen
We went for a walk with them
Sie haben uns eine tolle Geschichte erzählt
They told us a great story
Soll ich Ihnen etwas mitbringen?
Shall I bring something back for you?

3 Er hat es ihr gegeben
He gave it to her
Ich habe ihm ein neues Buch gekauft
I bought a new book for him/I bought him a new book

Personal Pronouns (ctd.)

- **du** is a singular form, used only when speaking to one person. It is used to talk to children, close friends and relatives, animals and objects of affection such as a toy, one's car etc.
  When in doubt it is always best to use the more formal **Sie** form.

- **ihr** is simply the plural form of **du** and is used in exactly the same situations wherever more than one person is to be addressed (→1)

- The familiar forms and their possessives are usually written with a small letter (→2)
  In letters however, they must begin with a capital letter (→3)

- **Sie** is the polite, or formal, way of addressing people. It is written in all its declined forms with a capital letter, including the possessive (→4)

  Sie is used:
  a) by children talking to adults outside their immediate family
  b) by adults talking to older children from mid-teens onwards. Teachers use it to their senior classes and bosses to their trainees etc.
  c) among adult strangers meeting for the first time
  d) among colleagues, friends and acquaintances unless a suggestion has been formally made by one party and accepted by the other that the familiar forms should be used. Familiar forms must then continue to be used at all times, as a reversion to the formal might be considered insulting.

Continued

1 Kinder, was wollt ihr essen?
Children, what do you want to eat?

2 Er hat mir gesagt, du sollst deine Frau mitbringen
He told me you were to bring your wife

3 Liebe Elke,
Gestern bin ich Deinem Bruder begegnet. Er wollte auch
mal wissen, warum Du nichts von Dir hören läßt!

Dear Elke,
I met your brother yesterday. He, too, was wondering why you
haven't been in touch!

4 Was haben Sie gesagt?
What did you say?

Ich habe es Ihnen schon gegeben
I have already given it to you

Ja, Ihre Sachen sind jetzt fertig
Yes, your things are ready now

Personal Pronouns (ctd.)

er/sie/es

All German nouns are masculine, feminine or neuter (→1)
The personal pronoun must agree in number and in gender
with the noun which it represents.

> **es** is used only for neuter nouns, and not for all inanimate
> objects (→2)
> Inanimate objects which are masculine use the pronoun
> **er** (→3)
> Feminine inanimate objects use the pronoun **sie** (→4)
> Neuter nouns referring to people have the neuter
> pronoun **es** (→5)

A common error for English speakers is to call all objects **es**.

man

This is used in much the same way as the pronoun **one** in
English, but it is much more commonly used in German (→6)
It is also used to make an alternative passive form (see p.34)
(→7)

The genitive personal pronoun

Genitive forms of the personal pronouns do exist (→8)
In practice however these are rarely used. Wherever possible,
alternative expressions are found which do not require the
genitive personal pronoun.

Special genitive forms exist for use with the prepositions
wegen and **willen** (→9)

Continued

1 **Der Tisch** the table (*masculine*)
Die Gardine the curtain (*feminine*)
Das Baby the baby (*neuter*)

2 **Das Bild ist schön** → **Es ist schön**
The picture is beautiful   → It is beautiful

3 **Der Tisch ist groß** → **Er ist groß**
The table is large   → It is large

4 **Die Gardine ist weiß** → **Sie ist weiß**
The curtain is white   → It is white

5 **Das Kind stand auf** → **Es stand auf**
The child stood up   → He/she stood up

6 **Es tut einem gut** It does one good

7 **Man holt mich um sieben ab**
I am being picked up at seven

8 | **meiner** of me | **unser** of us |
|---|---|
| **deiner** of you | **euer** of you (*plural*) |
| **seiner** of him/of it | **ihrer** of them |
| **ihrer** of her/it | **Ihrer** of you (*polite*) |

9 **meinetwegen** because of me, on my account
deinetwegen because of you, on your account *etc*
seinetwegen
ihretwegen
unsertwegen
euretwegen
Ihretwegen

meinetwillen for my sake, for me *etc*
deinetwillen
ihretwillen *etc*

Personal Pronouns (ctd.)

The use of pronouns after prepositions

- Personal pronouns used after prepositions and referring to a person are in the *case* required by the preposition in question (see p.198ff) (→**1**)

- When, however, a *thing* rather than a person is referred to, the construction:

    preposition + pronoun

    becomes:

    da- + *preposition* (→**2**) Before a preposition beginning with a vowel, the form: **dar-** + *preposition* is used (→**3**)

    This affects the following prepositions:

an	auf	aus
bei	durch	für
in	mit	nach
neben	über	unter
zwischen		

- These contracted forms are used after verbs followed by a preposition (see p.76ff) (→**4**)

- After prepositions used to express motion the form with **da(r)-** is not felt to be sufficiently strong. Forms with **hin** and **her** are used as follows:

aus :	heraus / hinaus
auf :	herauf / hinauf
in :	herein / hinein (→**4**)

1 **Ich bin mit ihm spazierengegangen**
   I went for a walk with him

2 **Klaus hatte ein Messer geholt und wollte damit den Kuchen
   aufschneiden**
   Klaus had brought a knife and was about to slice the cake with it

3 **Lege es bitte darauf**
   Put it on there please

4 **Der Unterschied liegt darin, daß ...**
   The difference is that ...
   Ich erinnere mich nicht daran
   I don't remember (it)

5 **Er sah eine Treppe und ging leise hinauf**
   He saw some stairs and climbed them quietly
   Endlich fand er unser Zelt und kam herein
   He finally found our tent and came in
   Er öffnete den Koffer und legte das Hemd hinein
   He opened his suitcase and put in his shirt

Possessive Pronouns

meiner mine
deiner yours
seiner his/its
ihrer hers/its
uns(e)rer ours
eu(e)rer yours (*plural*)
ihrer theirs
Ihrer yours (*polite form*)

These have the same endings as **dieser**. Their declension is therefore the same as for possessive adjectives (see p. 136) except in the masculine nominative singular and the neuter nominative and accusative singular:

	singular			plural
	masc	fem	neut	all genders
nom	**-ER**	**-e**	**-(E)S**	**-e**
acc	**-en**	**-e**	**-(E)S**	**-e**
gen	**-es**	**-er**	**-es**	**-er**
dat	**-em**	**-er**	**-em**	**-en**

● The bracketed **(e)** is often omitted, especially in spoken German

● Possessive pronouns must agree in number, gender and case with the noun they replace (→1)

● Note the translation of *of mine, of yours* etc (→2)

● **meiner** is declined in full opposite (→3)
Like **meiner** are **deiner**, **seiner** and **ihrer**.
Unserer and **euerer** are shown in full, since they have slightly different forms with an optional **-e-** (→4)

Continued

1 Der Wagen da drüben ist meiner. Er ist kleiner als deiner
   The car over there is mine. It is smaller than yours

2 Er ist ein Bekannter von mir
   He is an acquaintance of mine

3 meiner mine

	SINGULAR		PLURAL
MASC	FEM	NEUT	ALL GENDERS
meiner	**meine**	**mein(e)s**	**meine**
meinen	**meine**	**mein(e)s**	**meine**
meines	**meiner**	**meines**	**meiner**
meinem	**meiner**	**meinem**	**meinen**

4 uns(e)rer ours

	SINGULAR		PLURAL
MASC	FEM	NEUT	ALL GENDERS
uns(e)rer	**uns(e)re**	**uns(e)res**	**uns(e)re**
uns(e)ren	**uns(e)re**	**uns(e)res**	**uns(e)re**
uns(e)res	**uns(e)rer**	**uns(e)res**	**uns(e)rer**
uns(e)rem	**uns(e)rer**	**uns(e)rem**	**uns(e)ren**

eu(e)rer yours (*plural*)

	SINGULAR		PLURAL
MASC	FEM	NEUT	ALL GENDERS
eu(e)rer	**eu(e)re**	**euer(e)s**	**eu(e)re**
eu(e)ren	**eu(e)re**	**euer(e)s**	**eu(e)re**
eu(e)res	**eu(e)rer**	**eu(e)res**	**eu(e)rer**
eu(e)rem	**eu(e)rer**	**eu(e)rem**	**eu(e)ren**

Possessive Pronouns (ctd.)

Alternative forms

There are two alternatives to the **meiner/deiner** *etc* forms shown on p.167:

● der, die, das meinige mine
   der, die, das deinige yours
   der, die, das seinige his/its
   der, die, das ihrige hers/its
   der, die, das uns(e)rige ours
   der, die, das eu(e)rige yours (*plural*)
   der, die, das ihrige theirs
   der, die, das Ihrige yours (*polite form*)

These are almost as common as the **meiner/deiner** *etc* forms (→**1**)

These forms are declined as the definite article plus a weak adjective (see p.140) (→**2**)

The bracketed (**e**) of the first and second person plural is often omitted in spoken German.

● der, die, das meine mine
   der, die, das deine yours
   der, die, das seine his/its
   der, die, das ihre hers/its
   der, die, das uns(e)re ours
   der, die, das eu(e)re yours (*plural*)
   der, die, das ihre theirs
   der, die, das Ihre yours (*polite form*)

These forms are not as widely used as either of the previous two forms. They are declined as the definite article followed by a weak adjective (→**3**)

1 **Ihr Auto ist aber neuer als das meinige**
Your car is newer than mine
Paul hat seiner Freundin Blumen gekauft. Ich habe der meinigen Parfüm geschenkt
Paul bought his girlfriend some flowers. I bought mine perfume

2

	SINGULAR	
MASC	FEM	NEUT
der meinige	die meinige	das meinige
den meinigen	die meinige	das meinige
des meinigen	der meinigen	des meinigen
dem meinigen	der meinigen	dem meinigen

PLURAL
ALL GENDERS
die meinigen
die meinigen
der meinigen
den meinigen

3

	SINGULAR	
MASC	FEM	NEUT
der meine	die meine	das meine
den meinen	die meine	das meine
des meinen	der meinen	des meinen
dem meinen	der meinen	dem meinen

PLURAL
ALL GENDERS
die meinen
die meinen
der meinen
den meinen

Reflexive Pronouns

Reflexive pronouns, used to form reflexive verbs, have two forms, accusative and dative, as follows (→**1**)

ACCUSATIVE	DATIVE	
mich	**mir**	myself
dich	**dir**	yourself
sich	**sich**	himself/herself/ itself/themselves
uns	**uns**	ourselves
euch	**euch**	yourselves
sich	**sich**	yourself/yourselves (*polite forms*)

● Unlike personal pronouns and possessives, the polite forms have no capital letter (→**2**)

● For the position of reflexive pronouns within a sentence see p.30 (reflexive verbs) and pp.224 to 235 (sentence structure).

● Reflexive pronouns are also used after prepositions when the pronoun has the function of "reflecting back" to the subject of the sentence (→**3**)

● A further use of reflexive pronouns in German is with transitive verbs where the action is performed for the benefit of the subject, as in the English phrase:
I bought *myself* a new hat

The pronoun is not always translated in English (→**4**)

Continued

1 **Er hat sich rasiert** He had a shave
   Wir haben uns gebadet We had a bath
   Ich will es mir zuerst überlegen
   I'll have to think about it first

2 **Setzen Sie sich, bitte** Please take a seat

3 **Er hatte nicht genug Geld bei sich** (NOT **bei ihm**)
   He didn't have enough money on him

4 **Ich hole mir ein Bier**
   I'm going to get a beer (for myself)
   Er hat sich einen neuen Anzug gekauft
   He bought (himself) a new suit

Reflexive Pronouns (ctd.)

● Reflexive pronouns may be used for *reciprocal* actions, usually rendered by "each other" in English (→**1**)

Reciprocal actions may also be expressed by **einander**. This does not change in form (→**2**)

einander is always used in place of the reflexive pronoun after prepositions. Note that the preposition and **einander** come together to form one word (→**3**)

Emphatic reflexive pronouns

In English, these have the same forms as the normal reflexive pronouns:
    The queen *herself* has given the order
    I haven't read it *myself*, but ...

In German, this idea is expressed not by the reflexive pronouns, but by **selbst** or (in colloquial speech) **selber** placed at some point in the sentence after the noun or pronoun to which they refer (→**4**)

● **selbst/selber** do not change their form, regardless of number and gender of the noun to which they refer (→**4**)

● They are always stressed, regardless of their position in the sentence.

1 **Wir sind uns begegnet** We met (each other)
   Sie hatten sich auf einer Tagung kennengelernt
   They had got to know each other at a conference

2 **Wir kennen uns schon**
   OR:
   Wir kennen einander schon
   We already know each other

   Sie kennen sich schon
   OR:
   Sie kennen einander schon
   They already know each other

3 **Sie redeten miteinander**
   They were talking to each other

4 **Die Königin selbst hat es befohlen**
   The queen herself has given the order
   Ich habe es selbst nicht gelesen, aber ...
   I haven't read it myself, but ...

Relative Pronouns

These have the same forms as the definite article, except in the dative plural and genitive cases.

They are declined as follows:

	singular			plural
	masc	fem	neut	all genders
nom	**der**	**die**	**das**	**die**
acc	**den**	**die**	**das**	**die**
gen	**dessen**	**deren**	**dessen**	**deren**
dat	**dem**	**der**	**dem**	**denen**

- Relative pronouns must agree in gender and number with the noun to which they refer. They take their case however from the function they have in their own relative clause (→**1**)

- The relative pronoun cannot be omitted in German as it sometimes is in English (→**2**)

- The genitive forms are used in relative clauses in much the same way as in English (→**3**)
  Note however the translation of certain phrases (→**4**)

- When a preposition introduces the relative clause, the relative pronoun may be replaced by **wo-** or **wor-** if the noun or pronoun it stands for refers to an inanimate object or abstract concept (→**5**)
  The full form of relative pronoun plus preposition is however stylistically better.

- Relative clauses are always divided off by commas from the rest of the sentence (→**1-5**)

Continued

1 **Der Mann, den ich gestern gesehen habe, kommt aus Hamburg**
   The man whom I saw yesterday comes from Hamburg

2 **Die Frau, mit der ich gestern gesprochen habe, kennt deine Mutter**
   The woman I spoke to yesterday knows your mother

3 **Das Kind, dessen Fahrrad gestohlen worden war, ...**
   The child whose bicycle had been stolen ...

4 **Die Kinder, von denen einige schon lesen konnten, ...**
   The children, some of whom could read, ...
   Meine Freunden, von denen einer ...
   My friends, one of whom ...

5 **Der Zug, worauf wir warteten, hatte 20 Minuten Verspätung**
   OR:
   Der Zug, auf den wir warteten, hatte 20 Minuten Verspätung
   The train we were waiting for was running 20 minutes late

Relative Pronouns (ctd.)

welcher

A second relative pronoun exists. This has the same forms as the interrogative adjective **welcher** without the genitive forms:

	masc	singular fem	neut	plural all genders
nom	**welcher**	**welche**	**welches**	**welche**
acc	**welchen**	**welche**	**welches**	**welche**
gen	—	—	—	—
dat	**welchem**	**welcher**	**welchem**	**welchen**

- These forms are used only infrequently as relative pronouns, where sentence rhythm might benefit.

- They are also useful used as articles or adjectives to connect a noun in the relative clause with the contents of the main clause (→1)

wer, was

These are normally used as interrogative pronouns meaning *who?*, *what?* and are declined as such on p.178.

- They may however also be used without interrogative meaning to replace both subject and relative pronoun in English:
  he who, a woman who, anyone who, those who etc (→2)

- **was** is the relative pronoun used in set expressions with certain neuter forms (→3)

1 **Er glaubte, mit der Hausarbeit nicht helfen zu brauchen, mit welcher Idee seine Mutter nicht einverstanden war!**
He thought he didn't have to help in the house, an idea with which his mother was not in agreement!

2 **Wer das glaubt, ist verrückt**
Anyone who believes that is mad
Was mich angeht, ... For my part ...
Was du gestern gekauft hast, steht dir ganz gut
The things you bought yesterday suit you very well

3 **nichts, was ...** nothing that
  vieles, was... a lot that
  einiges, was ... some that
  dasselbe, was ... the same one that
  wenig, was ... little that
  dasjenige, was ... that which
  folgendes, was ... the following which
  manches, was ... some which
  allerlei, was ... all kinds of things that
  alles, was ... everything which
  das, was ... that which

  Nichts, was er sagte, hat gestimmt
Nothing that he said was right
Das, was du jetzt machst, ist reiner Unsinn!
What you are doing now is sheer nonsense!
Mit allem, was du mitgebracht hast, kommen wir gut aus
We'll manage very well on everything that you've brought

Interrogative Pronouns

These are the pronouns used to ask questions.

As in English, they have few forms, singular and plural being the same.

They are declined as follows:

	persons	things
nom	**wer?**	**was?**
acc	**wen?**	**was?**
gen	**wessen?**	**wessen?**
dat	**wem?**	—

- They are used in direct questions (→**1**) or in indirect questions (→**2**)

- When used as the subject of a sentence, they are always followed by a singular verb (→**3**)
  EXCEPTION:
  When followed by a verb and taking a noun complement, the verb may be plural if the sense demands it (→**4**)

- The interrogative pronouns can be used in rhetorical questions or in exclamations (→**5**)

Continued

1 **Wer hat es gemacht?** Who did it?
   Mit wem bist du gekommen?
   Who did you come with?

2 **Ich weiß nicht, wer es gemacht hat**
   I don't know who did it
   Er wollte wissen, mit wem er fahren sollte
   He wanted to know who he was to travel with

3 **Wer kommt heute?** Who's coming today?

4 **Wer sind diese Leute?** Who are these people?

5 **Was haben wir gelacht!** How we laughed!

Interrogative Pronouns (ctd.)

● When used with prepositions, **was** usually becomes **wo-** and is placed in front of the preposition to form one word with it (**→1**)
Where the preposition begins with a vowel, **wor-** is used instead (**→2**)
This construction is similar to **da(r)-** + *preposition* shown on p.164

As with **da(r)-** + *preposition*, this construction is not used when the preposition is intended to convey movement. **Wohin** (*where to*) and **woher** (*where from*) are used instead (**→3**)

was für ein?, welcher?

● These are used to mean *what kind of one?* and *which one?*

● They are declined as shown on pp.124 and 128.

● They are used to form either direct or indirect questions (**→4**)

● They may refer either to persons or to things with the appropriate declension endings (**→5**)

1 Wonach sehnst du dich? What do you long for?
Wodurch ist es zerstört worden?
How was it destroyed?

2 Worauf kann man sich heutzutage noch verlassen?
What is there left to rely on these days?

3 Wohin fährst du? Where are you going?
Woher kommt das?
Where has this come from?/How has this come about?

4 Was für eins hat er?
What kind (of one) does he have?
Welches hast du gewollt?
Which one did you want?

5 Für welchen hat sie sich entschieden?
Which one (*man/hat etc*) did she choose?

Indefinite Pronouns

jemand someone, somebody

nom **jemand**
acc **jemanden, jemand**
gen **jemand(e)s**
dat **jemandem, jemand** (→1)

niemand no one, nobody

nom **niemand**
acc **niemanden, niemand**
gen **niemand(e)s**
dat **niemandem, niemand** (→2)

● The forms without endings are used in conversational German, but the inflected forms are preferred in literary and written styles.

● When **niemand** and **jemand** are used with a following adjective, they are usually not declined, but the adjective takes a capital letter and is declined as follows:

nom **jemand/niemand Gutes**
acc **jemand/niemand Gutes**
gen —
dat **jemand/niemand Gutem** (→3)

● When **jemand** and **niemand** are followed by **ander(e)s**, this is written with a small letter, e.g. **jemand/niemand ander(e)s**.

Continued

1 Ich habe es jemandem (*dat*) **gegeben**
I gave it to someone

Irgend jemand (*nom*) **hat es genommen**
Someone or other has stolen it

2 Er hat niemanden (*acc*) **gesehen**
He didn't see anyone

Er ist unterwegs niemandem (*dat*) **begegnet**
He encountered no-one on the way

3 Diese Aufgabe braucht jemand Intelligentes
Someone intelligent is needed for this task

Indefinite Pronouns (ctd.)

keiner none

	singular			plural
	masc	fem	neut	all genders
nom	**keiner**	**keine**	**keins**	**keine**
acc	**keinen**	**keine**	**keins**	**keine**
dat	**keinem**	**keiner**	**keinem**	**keinen**

- It is declined like the article **kein, keine, kein** (see p.126) except in the nominative masculine and nominative and accusative neuter forms (→**1**)

- It may be used to refer to people or things (→**1**)

einer one

	singular		
	masc	fem	neut
nom	**einer**	**eine**	**ein(e)s**
acc	**einen**	**eine**	**ein(e)s**
gen	**eines**	**einer**	**eines**
dat	**einem**	**einer**	**einem**

- This pronoun may be used to refer to either persons or things (→**2**)

- It exists only in the singular forms.

Continued

1 Keiner von ihnen hat es tun können
Not one of them was able to do it

Gibst du mir eine Zigarette? — Tut mir leid, ich habe keine
Will you give me a cigarette? — Sorry, I haven't got any

2 Sie ist mit einem meiner Verwandten verlobt
She is engaged to one of my relatives

Wo sind die anderen Kinder? Ich sehe hier nur eins
Where are the rest of the children? I can only see one here

Gibst du mir einen? (e.g. einen Bonbon, einen Zehner *etc*)
Gibst du mir eine? (e.g. eine Zigarette, eine Blume *etc*)
Gibst du mir eins? (e.g. ein Buch, ein Butterbrot *etc*)
Will you give me one?

Indefinite Pronouns (ctd.)

- Certain adjectives and articles can be used as pronouns.

- The following are all declined to agree in gender and number with the noun or pronoun they represent (→1):

  mehrere several
  ander other

  derjenige that one
  derselbe the same one

  mancher some
  jeder each (one), every one
  jener that one
  dieser this one
  solcher such as that, such a one
  mancher some, quite a few
  einiger some
  welcher which one
  aller all
  irgendwelcher someone or other; something or other
  beide both
  sämtliche all, the lot

- The following do not change whatever the gender or number of the noun or pronoun they represent (→2):

etwas some, something	**nichts** nothing, none
ein paar a few	**ein wenig** a little, a few
mehr more	**ein bißchen** a bit, a little

- When an adjective follows **etwas** or **nichts**, it takes a capital letter and declension endings: **etwas/nichts Gutes** something/nothing good.

1 Andere machen es besser (e.g. **Leute, Waschmaschinen** *etc*)
Others do it better

Mit einem solchen kommst du nicht nach Hause (e.g. **Wagen** *etc*)
You won't make it home in one like that

Alles, was er ihr schenkte, schickte sie sofort zurück
Everything that he gave her she sent back at once

Er war mit beiden zufrieden (e.g. **Computern, Autos** *etc*)
He was satisfied with both

2 Ich muß dir etwas sagen
I must tell you something

Etwas ist herausgefallen
Something fell out

Nichts ist geschehen
Nothing happened

Er ist mit nichts zufrieden
He is content with nothing

Gibst du mir bitte ein paar?
Will you give me a few?

Er hatte ein wenig bei sich
He had a little with him

Er braucht immer mehr, um zu leben
He needs more and more to live

Use of adverbs

● Adverbs, or phrases which are used as adverbs, may:

    a) modify a verb (→**1**)

    b) modify an adjective (→**2**)

    c) modify another adverb (→**3**)

    d) modify a conjunction (→**4**)

    e) ask a question (→**5**)

    f) form verb prefixes (see p.72) (→**6**)

● Adverbs are also used, in much the same way as in English, to make the meaning of certain tenses more precise e.g.

    a) with continuous tenses (→**7**)

    b) to show a future meaning where the tense used is not future (→**8**)

Continued

1 **Er ging langsam über die Brücke**
He walked slowly over the bridge

2 **Er ist ein ziemlich großer Kerl**
He's quite a big chap

3 **Sie arbeitet heute besonders tüchtig**
She's working exceptionally well today

4 **Wenn er es nur aufgeben wollte!**
If only he would give it up!

5 **Wann kommt er an?**
When does he arrive?

6 **falsch spielen** to cheat (*at cards*)
hintragen to carry (*to a place*)

7 **Er liest gerade die Zeitung**
He's just reading the paper

8 **Er wollte gerade aufstehen, als ...**
He was just about to get up when ...

Wir fahren morgen nach Köln
We're driving to Cologne tomorrow

The Formation of Adverbs

- Many adverbs are simply adjectives used as adverbs. Used in this way, unlike adjectives, they are not declined (→1)

- Some adverbs are formed by adding **-weise** or **-sweise** to a noun (→2)

- Some adverbs are also formed by adding **-erweise** to an uninflected adjective.
  Such adverbs are used mainly to show the speaker's opinion (→3)

- There is also a class of adverbs which are not formed from other parts of speech e.g.
      unten, oben, leider (→4)
  and those shown in the paragraphs below.

- For the position of adverbs within a clause or sentence, see the section on sentence structure, pp.224 to 235.

- The following are some common adverbs of time:
      morgen tomorrow
      morgens in the mornings
      heute today
      endlich finally
      sofort at once
      immer always   (→5)

- The following are some common adverbs of degree:
      äußerst extremely
      besonders especially
      ziemlich fairly
      beträchtlich considerably   (→6)

Continued

1 **Habe ich das richtig gehört?**
Is it true what I've heard?

    Sie war modern angezogen
    She was fashionably dressed

2 **beispielsweise** for example
    beziehungsweise or; or rather; that is to say
    schrittweise step by step
    zeitweise at times
    zwangsweise compulsorily

3 **glücklicherweise** fortunately
    komischerweise strangely enough
    erstaunlicherweise astonishingly enough

4 **Unten wohnte Frau Schmidt**
Mrs. Smith lived downstairs

    Leider können wir nicht kommen
    Unfortunately we cannot come

5 **Ich kann erst morgen kommen**
I can't come till tomorrow

    Das Kind hat immer Hunger
    The child is always hungry

6 **Das Paket war besonders schwer**
The parcel was unusually heavy

    Diese Übung ist ziemlich leicht
    This exercise is quite easy

Adverbs of place

In certain respects German adverbs of place behave very differently from their English counterparts:

● Where no movement, or movement within the same place, is involved, the adverb is used in its simple dictionary form (→**1**)

● Movement *away from the speaker* is shown by the presence of **hin** (→**2**)
The following compound adverbs are therefore often used when movement away from the original position is concerned, even though a simple adverb would be used in English:

wohin? where (to)?
irgendwohin (to) somewhere or other
überallhin everywhere
dahin (to) there
hierhin here
dorthin there   (→**3**)

● Movement *towards the speaker* or central person is shown by the presence of **her**.
The following compound adverbs are therefore much used to show movement towards a person:

woher? where from?
hierher here
irgendwoher from somewhere or other
daher from there
überallher from all over   (→**4**)

Continued

1 **Wo ist er?** Where is he?
Er ist nicht da He isn't there

Hier darf man nicht parken
You can't park here

2 **Klaus und Ulli geben heute eine Party. Gehen wir hin?**
Klaus and Ulli are giving a party today. Shall we go?

3 **Wohin fährst du?** Where are you going?

Sie liefen überallhin They ran everywhere

4 **Woher kommst du?** Where do you come from?

Woher hast du das? Where did you get that from?

Das habe ich irgendwoher gekriegt
I got that from somewhere or other

Comparison of Adverbs

- The **comparative** form of the adverb is obtained in exactly the same way as that of adjectives, i.e. by adding **-er** (→1)

- The **superlative** form is formed as follows:
     am + *adverb* + **-sten/-esten**
  It is not declined (→2)

- Note the use of the comparative adverb with **immer** to show progression (→3)

- *the more ... the more ...* is expressed in German by **je ... desto ...** or **je ... um so ...** (→4)

- Some adverbial superlatives are used to show the extent of a quality rather than a comparison with others. These are as follows:
     spätestens *at the latest*
     höchstens *at the most; at best*
     wenigstens *at least*
     meistens *mostly; most often*
     strengstens *strictly, absolutely*
     bestens *very well; very warmly*   (→5)

- Two irregular comparatives and superlatives:
  gern → lieber → am liebsten (used with **haben**)
  well → better → best

  bald → eher → am ehesten
  soon → sooner → soonest   (→6)

1 Er läuft schneller als seine Schwester
He runs faster than his sister

Ich sehe ihn seltener als früher
I see him less often than before

2 Wer von ihnen arbeitet am schnellsten?
Which of them works fastest?

Er ißt am meisten He eats most

3 Die Mädchen sprachen immer lauter
The girls were talking more and more loudly

Er fuhr immer langsamer
He drove more and more slowly

4 Je eher, desto besser The sooner the better

5 Er kommt meistens zu spät an
He usually arrives late

Rauchen strengstens verboten!
No smoking

6 Welches hast du am liebsten?
Which do you like best?

Emphasizers

These are words commonly used in German, as indeed in English, especially in the spoken language, to emphasize or modify in some way the meaning of the sentence. The following are some of the most common:

aber
Used to lend emphasis to a statement (→1)

denn
As well as its uses as a conjunction (see p.214), **denn** is widely used to emphasize the meaning. It often cannot be directly translated (→2)

doch
Is used as a positive reply in order to correct negative assumptions or impressions (→3)

It can strengthen an imperative (→4)

It can make a question out of a statement (→5)

mal
May be used with imperatives (→6)

It also has several idiomatic uses (→7)

ja
Strengthens a statement (→8)

It also has several idiomatic uses (→9)

schon
Is used familiarly with an imperative (→10)

It is also used in various idiomatic ways (→11)

1 Das ist aber schön! Oh that's pretty!
  Aber doch! Yes indeed!

2 Was ist denn hier los?
  What's going on here then?
  Wo denn? Where?

3 Hat es dir nicht gefallen? — Doch!
  Didn't you like it? — Oh yes, I did!

4 Laß ihn doch! Just leave him

5 Das schaffst du doch?
  You'll manage it, won't you?

6 Komm mal her! Come here!
  Moment mal! Just a minute!

7 Mal sehen We'll see
  Er soll es nur mal versuchen!
  Just let him try it!
  Hören Sie mal ... Look here now ...

8 Er sieht ja wie seine Mutter aus
  He looks like his mother
  Das kann ja sein That may well be

9 Ja und? So what?/What then?
  Das ist ja lächerlich That's ridiculous
  Das ist es ja That's just it

10 Laß schon! Let it be!/Leave it alone!

11 Wenn schon! What of it?/So what?
  Schon gut Okay /Very well

Prepositions

In English, a preposition does not affect the word or phrase which it introduces e.g.

the women / a large meal / these events
with the women / *after* a large meal / *before* these events

In German, however, the noun following a preposition must be put in a certain *case*: accusative (→**1**)
dative (→**2**)
genitive (→**3**)
It is therefore important to learn each preposition with the case, or cases, it governs.

The following guidelines will help you:

- Prepositions which take the accusative or dative cases are much more common than those taking the genitive case.

- Certain prepositions may take a dative or accusative case, depending on whether *movement* is involved or not. This is explained further on pp.202 ff. (→**4**)

- Prepositions are often used to complete the sense of certain verbs, as shown on p.76ff (→**5**)

- After many prepositions, a shortened or *contracted* form of the definite article may be merged with the preposition to form one word, e.g.

auf + das   becomes **aufs**
bei + dem   becomes **beim**
zu + der   becomes **zur**

Continued

1 **Es ist für dich**
   It's for you
   Wir sind durch die ganze Welt gereist
   We travelled all over the world

2 **Er ist mit seiner Frau gekommen**
   He came with his wife

3 **Es ist ihm trotz seiner Bemühungen mißlungen**
   Despite his efforts, he still didn't succeed

4 **Es liegt auf dem Tisch**
   It's on the table (*dative*: no movement implied)
   Lege es bitte auf den Tisch Please put it on the table
   (*accusative*: movement *onto* the table)

5 **Ich warte auf meinen Mann**
   I'm waiting for my husband

Prepositions: contracted forms (ctd.)

Such contractions are possible with the following prepositions:

preposition	+ das	+ den	+ dem	+ der
hinter	hinters*	hintern*	hinterm*	
über	übers*	übern*	überm*	
unter	unters*	untern*	unterm*	
zu			zum	zur
an	ans		am	
vor	vors*		vorm*	
in	ins		im	
bei			beim	
von			vom	
durch	durchs*			
für	fürs*			
auf	aufs*			
um	ums*			

- Those forms marked with an asterisk are suitable only for use in colloquial, spoken German.
  All other forms (not marked with an asterisk) may be safely used in any context, formal or informal (→1)

- Contracted forms are obviously not used where the article is to be stressed (→2)

- Other contracted forms involving prepositions, as shown on p.164 and 174, occur:
  1) in the introduction to relative clauses (→3)
  2) with personal pronouns representing inanimate objects (→4)

Continued

1 Wir gehen heute Abend ins Theater
We are going to the theatre this evening

Er geht zur Schule
He goes to school

Das kommt vom Trinken
That comes from drinking

2 In die Schule geht mein Sohn aber nicht!
My son is certainly not going to that school!

3 Die Bank, worauf wir saßen, war etwas wackelig
The bench we were sitting on was somewhat wobbly

4 Er war damit zufrieden
He was satisfied with that

Er hat es darauf gesetzt
He put it on it

Prepositions followed by the Dative Case

Some of the most common prepositions taking the dative case are:

aus	gegenüber	seit
außer	mit	von
bei	nach	zu

aus

- as a preposition meaning *out of/from* (→1)

- as a separable verbal prefix (see p.72) (→2)

außer

- as a preposition meaning: *out of* (→3)
  except (→4)

bei

- as a preposition meaning: *at the home/shop/work (etc) of* (→5)
  near (→6)
  in the course of/during (→7)

- as a separable verbal prefix (see p.72) (→8)

gegenüber

- as a preposition meaning: *opposite* (→9)
  to(wards) (→10)

  NOTE: when used as a preposition, **gegenüber** is placed *after a pronoun*, but may be placed *before or after a noun*

- as a separable verbal prefix (→11)

Continued

1 Er trinkt aus der Flasche
He is drinking out of the bottle
Er kommt aus Essen He comes from Essen

2 aushalten to endure →
Ich halte es nicht mehr aus
I can't stand it any longer

3 außer Gefahr/Betrieb out of danger/order

4 alle außer mir all except me

5 Bei uns in Schottland
At home in Scotland
Er wohnt immer noch bei seinen Eltern
He still lives with his parents

6 Er saß bei mir ...
He was sitting next to me
Ich singe immer beim Arbeiten
I always sing when I'm working

7 Bei unserer Ankunft ...
On our arrival ...

8 Er stand seinem Freund bei
He stood by his friend

9 Er wohnt uns gegenüber
He lives opposite us

10 Er ist mir gegenüber immer sehr freundlich gewesen
He has always been very friendly towards me

11 gegenüberstehen to face/to have an attitude towards →
Er steht ihnen kritisch gegenüber
He takes a critical view of them

Prepositions followed by the Dative Case
(ctd.)

mit
- as a preposition meaning *with* (→**1**)
- as a separable verbal prefix (see p.72) (→**2**)

nach
- as a preposition meaning: *after* (→**3**)
  to (→**4**)
  according to (it can be placed after the noun with this meaning (→**5**)
- as a separable verbal prefix (see p.72) (→**6**)

seit
- a preposition meaning: *since* (→**7**)
  for (of time; note the tense!) (→**8**)

von
- as a preposition meaning: *from* (→**9**)
  about (→**10**)
- as an alternative, often preferred, to the genitive case (→**11**)
- meaning *by*, to introduce the agent of a passive action (see p.34) (→**12**)

zu
- as a preposition meaning: *to* (→**13**)
  for (→**14**)
- as a separable verbal prefix (see p.72) (→**15**)

Continued

1 Er ging mit seinen Freunden spazieren
He went walking with his friends

2 jemanden mitnehmen to give somone a lift →
Nimmst du mich bitte mit?
Will you give me a lift please?

3 Nach zwei Stunden kam er wieder
He returned two hours later

4 Er ist nach London gereist
He went to London

5 Ihrer Sprache nach ist sie Süddeutsche
From her speech I would say she is from southern Germany

6 nachmachen to copy →
Sie macht mir alles nach
She copies everything I do

7 Seit der Zeit ...
Since then ...

8 Ich wohne seit zwei Jahren in Frankfurt
I've been living in Frankfurt for two years

9 Von Frankfurt sind wir weiter nach München gefahren
From Frankfurt we went on to Munich

10 Ich weiß nichts von ihm
I know nothing about him

11 Die Mutter von diesen Mädchen ...
The mother of these girls ...
Sie ist eine Freundin von Peter
She is a friend of Peter's

12 Er ist von unseren Argumenten überzeugt worden
He was convinced by our arguments

13 Er ging zum Arzt
He went to the doctor's

14 Wir sind zum Essen eingeladen
We're invited for dinner

15 zumachen to shut →
Mach die Tür zu
Shut the door

Prepositions followed by the Accusative Case

The most common of these are:

> durch   für   ohne   wider
> entlang gegen um

durch

- as a preposition meaning *through* (→1)
- preceding the inanimate agent of a passive action (see p.34) (→2)
- as a separable verbal prefix

entlang

- as a preposition meaning *along*, in which case it follows the noun (→3)
- as a separable verbal prefix (→4)

für

- as a preposition meaning: *for* (→5)
-                            *to* (→6)
- in **was für/was für ein** *what kind of/what*, as shown on p.144 and p.180) (→7)

gegen

- as a preposition meaning: *against* (→8)
-                           *towards/getting on for* (→9)
- as a separable verbal prefix

Continued

1 durch das Fenster blicken
to look through the window

2 Durch seine Bemühungen wurden alle gerettet
Everyone was saved through his efforts

3 die Straße entlang
along the street

4 die Straße entlanggehen
to go along the street

5 Ich habe es für dich getan
I did it for you

6 Das ist für ihn sehr wichtig
That is very important to him

7 Was für Äpfel sind das?
What kind of apples are they?

8 Stelle es gegen die Mauer
Put it against the wall
Haben Sie ein Mittel gegen Schnupfen?
Have you something for (= against) colds?
Ich habe nichts dagegen
I've got nothing against it

9 Wir sind gegen vier angekommen
We arrived around/at getting on for four o'clock

Prepositions followed by the Accusative Case (ctd.)

ohne

● as a preposition meaning *without* (→1)

um

● as a preposition meaning: (a)round/round about (→2)
  at (in time expressions) (→3)
  for (after certain verbs) (→4)
  about (after certain verbs) (→5)
  by (in expressions of quantity) (→6)

● as a variable verbal prefix (see p.74) (→7)

wider

● as a preposition meaning *contrary to/against* (→8)

● as a variable verbal prefix (see p.74) (→9)

Continued

1 Ohne ihn geht's nicht
It won't work without him

2 um die Ecke (a)round the corner

3 Es fängt um neun Uhr an It begins at nine

4 Sie baten ihre Mutter um Kekse
They asked their mother for some biscuits

5 Es handelt sich um dein Benehmen
It's a question of your behaviour

6 Es ist um zehn Mark billiger
It is cheaper by ten marks

7 umarmen to embrace (*inseparable*) →
Er hat sie umarmt
He gave her a hug

umfallen to fall over (*separable*) →
Er ist umgefallen
He fell over

8 Das geht mir wider die Natur
That's against my nature

9 widersprechen to go against (*inseparable*) →
Das hat meinen Wünschen widersprochen
That went against my wishes

widertönen to echo (*separable*) →
Seine Worte tönte ihr noch im Ohr wider
His words were still ringing in her ears

Prepositions followed by the Dative or the Accusative

These prepositions are followed by:

the **accusative** when *movement towards* a different place is involved

the **dative** when *position* is described as opposed to movement, or when the movement is *within* the same place.

- The most common prepositions in this category are:

  in *in/into/to* (→1)
  an *on/at/to*
  auf *on/in/to/at*
  unter *under/among* (→2)
  über *over/across/above*
  vor *in front of/before*
  hinter *behind*
  neben *next to/beside*
  zwischen *between* (→3)

- These prepositions may also be used with figurative meanings as part of a *verb + preposition* construction (see p.76).
  The case following **auf** or **an** is then not the same after all verbs (→4)
  It is therefore best to learn such constructions together with the case which follows them.

- Many of these prepositions are also used as verb prefixes in the same way as the prepositions described on pp.202 to 209 (→5)

Continued

1 **Er ging ins Zimmer** (*acc*)
He entered the room

Im Zimmer (*dat*) **warteten viele Leute auf ihn**
A lot of people were waiting for him in the room

2 **Er rannte unter das Dach** (*acc*)
He ran in under the roof

Er lebte dort unter Freunden (*dat*)
There he lived among friends

3 **Er legte es zwischen die beiden Teller** (*acc*)
He put it between the two plates

Das Dorf liegt zwischen den Bergen (*dat*)
The village lies between the mountains

4 **sich verlassen auf** (+ *acc*) to depend on
bestehen auf (+ *dat*) to insist on

glauben an (+ *acc*) to believe in
leiden an (+ *dat*) to suffer from

5 **anrechnen** to charge for (*separable*) →
Das wird Ihnen später angerechnet
You'll be charged for that later

aufsetzen to put on (*separable*) →
Sie setzte sich den Hut auf
She put her hat on

überqueren to cross (*inseparable*) →
Sie hat die Straße überquert
She crossed the street

Prepositions followed by the Genitive Case

The following are some of the more common prepositions which take the genitive case:

diesseits *on this side of*
jenseits *on the other side of* (→1)
beiderseits *on both sides of*
innerhalb *within/inside* (→2)
außerhalb *outside*
während* *during* (→3)
statt* *instead of*
trotz* *in spite of* (→4)
wegen* *on account of* (→5)
infolge *as a result of*
hinsichtlich *with regard to*
... halber *for ... sake/because of ...*
um ... willen *for ... sake/because of ...*

- Those prepositions marked with an asterisk may also be followed by the dative case (→6)

- Note that special forms of the possessive and relative pronouns are used with **wegen, halber** and **willen** (→7)

1 **jenseits der Grenze**
  on the other side of the frontier

2 **innerhalb dieses Zeitraums**
  within this period of time

3 **während der Vorstellung**
  during the performance

4 **trotz seiner Befürchtungen**
  despite his apprehensions

5 **wegen der neuen Stelle**
  because of the new job

6 **trotz allem** in spite of everything
  wegen mir because of me

7 **meinetwegen** on my account, because of me
  deinetwegen on your account, because of you
  seinetwegen on his account, because of him
  ihretwegen on her/their account, because of her/them
  unsertwegen on our account, because of us
  euertwegen on your account, because of you
  Ihretwegen on your account, because of you (*polite*)
  derentwegen for whose sake, for her/their/its sake
  dessentwegen for whose sake, for his/its sake

  meinethalben *etc* on my *etc* account
  derenthalben on whose account, on her/their/its account
  dessenthalben on whose account, on his/its account

  meinetwillen *etc* for my *etc* sake
  derentwillen for whose sake, for her/its/their sake
  dessentwillen for whose sake, for his/its sake

Co-ordinating Conjunctions

These are used to link words, phrases or clauses (→1)

● These are the main co-ordinating conjunctions:

      und and (→1)

      oder or (→2)

      aber but (→3)
            however (→4)

      denn for (→5)

      sondern but (after a negative construction) (→6)

● These do not cause subject-verb inversion, i.e. the verb follows the subject in the normal way (see p.224) (→1-6)

● Inversion may however be caused by something other than the co-ordinating conjunction, e.g. **dann**, **trotzdem**, **montags** in the examples opposite (→7)

● When used with the meaning of *however*, **aber** is placed within the clause, and not at the beginning (→4)

● When linked by co-ordinating conjunctions, no comma is required between clauses (cf. p.240).

Continued

1 **Peter und Veronika** Peter and Veronika
   Er ging in die Stadt und kaufte sich ein neues Hemd
   He went into town and bought himself a new shirt

2 **Er hatte noch nie Whisky oder Schnaps getrunken**
   He had never drunk whisky or schnapps
   Willst du eins, oder hast du vielleicht keinen Hunger?
   Do you want one or aren't you hungry?

3 **Wir wollten ins Kino, aber wir hatten kein Geld**
   We wanted to go to the cinema but we had no money

4 **Ich wollte ins Theater; er aber wollte nicht mit**
   I wanted to go to the theatre; however he wouldn't come

5 **Wir wollten heute fahren, denn montags ist weniger Verkehr**
   We wanted to travel today because the traffic is lighter on
   Mondays

6 **Er ist nicht alt, sondern jung**
   He isn't old, but young

7 **Er hat sie besucht, und dann ist er wieder nach Hause
   gegangen**
   He paid her a visit and then went home again
   **Wir wollten doch ins Kino, aber trotzdem sind wir zu Hause
   geblieben**
   We wanted to go to the cinema, but even so stayed at home
   Wir wollten heute fahren, denn montags ist weniger Verkehr
   We wanted to travel today, because there is less traffic on
   Mondays

Double Co-ordinating Conjunctions

These conjunctions consist of two separate elements, like their
English counterparts e.g.

not only ... but also ...

The following are widely used:

sowohl ... als (auch) *both ... and*

- This may link words or phrases (→1)

- The verb is usually plural, whether the subjects are singular
  or plural (→1)

weder ... noch *neither ... nor*

- This may link words or phrases (→2)

- It may also link clauses, and inversion of subject and verb
  then takes place in both clauses (→3)

- The verb is plural unless both subjects are singular (→4)

Continued

1 **Sowohl sein Vater als auch seine Mutter haben sich darüber gefreut**
   Both his father and his mother were pleased about it
   Sowohl unser Lehrkörper als auch unsere Schüler haben teilgenommen
   Both our staff and our pupils took part

2 **Weder Georg noch sein Bruder kannte das Mädchen**
   Neither George nor his brother knew the girl

3 **Weder mag ich ihn, noch respektiere ich ihn**
   I neither like nor respect him

4 **Weder die Damen noch die Herren haben recht**
   Neither the ladies nor the gentlemen are right
   Weder du noch ich würde es schaffen
   Neither you nor I would be able to do it

Double Co-ordinating Conjunctions (ctd.)

nicht nur ... sondern auch *not only ... but also*

- This is used to link clauses as well as words and phrases (→**1**)

- The word order is: inversion of subject and verb in the first clause, and normal order in the second (→**2**)
  However, if **nicht nur** does not begin the clause, normal order prevails (→**3**)

- The verb agrees in number with the subject nearest to it (→**4**)

entweder ... oder *either ... or*

- The verb agrees with the subject nearest it (→**5**)

- The normal word order is: inversion in the first clause, and normal order in the second (→**6**)
  However, it is possible to use normal order in the first clause, and this lends a threatening tone to the statement (→**7**)

teils ... teils *partly ... partly*

- The verb is normally plural unless both subjects are singular (→**8**)

- Inversion of subject and verb takes place in both clauses (→**9**)

1 **Er ist nicht nur geschickt, sondern auch intelligent**
   Nicht nur ist er geschickt, sondern er ist auch intelligent
   He is not only skilful but also intelligent

2 **Nicht nur hat es die ganze Zeit geregnet, sondern ich habe**
   mir auch noch das Bein gebrochen
   Not only did it rain the whole time, but I also broke my leg

3 **Es hat nicht nur die ganze Zeit geregnet, sondern ich habe**
   mir auch noch das Bein gebrochen
   Not only did it rain the whole time, but I also broke my leg

4 **Nicht nur ich, sondern auch die Mädchen sind dafür**
   verantwortlich
   Not just me, but the girls too are responsible
   Nicht nur sie, sondern auch ich habe es gehört
   It wasn't only they who heard it — I heard it too

5 **Entweder du oder Georg muß es getan haben**
   It must have been either you or George who did it

6 **Entweder komme ich morgen vorbei, oder ich ruf dich an**
   I'll either drop in tomorrow or I'll give you a ring

7 **Entweder du gibst sofort auf, oder du kriegst kein**
   Taschengeld mehr
   Either you give it up immediately, or you get no more pocket
   money

8 **Die Studenten waren teils Deutsche, teils Ausländer**
   The students were partly German and partly from abroad

9 **Teils bin ich überzeugt, teils bleib ich skeptisch**
   A bit of me is convinced, and a bit remains sceptical

Subordinating Conjunctions

These are used to link clauses in such a way as to make one clause dependent on another for its meaning. The dependent clause is called a **subordinate clause** and the other a **main clause**.

- The subordinate clause is always separated from the rest of the sentence by commas (→1)

- The subordinate clause may precede the main clause. When this happens, the verb and subject of the main clause are inverted i.e. they swap places, as shown on p.226 (→2)

- The finite part of the verb (i.e. the conjugated part) is always at the end of a subordinate clause (see p.228) (→3)

- For compound tenses in subordinate clauses, it is the **auxiliary** (the main part of the verb) which comes last, after the participle or infinitive used to form the compound tense (see the section on compound tenses) (→4)

- Any **modal verb (mögen, können** etc. — p.52ff) used in a subordinate clause is placed last in the clause (→5)

  EXCEPTION: when the modal verb is in a compound tense, the order is as shown (→6)

Continued

MAIN CLAUSE   SUBORDINATE CLAUSE

1 **Er ist zu Fuß gekommen, weil der Bus zu teuer ist**
He came on foot because the bus is too dear
Ich trinke viel Bier, obwohl es nicht gesund ist
I drink a lot of beer although it isn't good for me
Wir haben weiter gefeiert, nachdem sie gegangen waren
We carried on the party after they went

SUBORDINATE CLAUSE   MAIN CLAUSE

2 **Weil der Bus zu teuer ist, geht er zu Fuß**
Obwohl es nicht gesund ist, trinke ich viel Bier
Nachdem sie gegangen waren, haben wir weiter gefeiert

3 **Als er uns sah, ist er davongelaufen**
Er ist davongelaufen, als er uns sah
He ran away when he saw us

4 **Nachdem er gegessen hatte, ging er hinaus**
He went out after he had eaten

5 **Da er mit uns nicht sprechen wollte, ist er davongelaufen**
Since he didn't want to speak to us he ran away

6 **Da er nicht mit uns hat sprechen wollen, ist er davongelaufen**
Since he didn't want to speak to us, he ran away

Subordinating conjunctions (ctd.)

● Here are some common examples of subordinating conjunctions and their uses:

>**nachdem** after (→**1**)
>**indem** while
>**wenn** when/whenever; if (→**2**)
>**als** when (→**3**)
>**wann** when (*interrogative*) (→**4**)
>**während** while (→**5**)
>**bevor** before
>**sobald** as soon as
>**wohin** to where
>**worin** in which
>**inwiefern** to what extent
>**soweit** as far as
>**worauf** whereupon; on which
>**als ob** as if/as though
>**weil** because
>**seitdem** since
>**bis** until (→**6**)
>**wo** where
>**wie** as/like
>**da** as/since (→**7**)
>**obwohl** although
>**damit** so (that) (→**8**)
>**so daß** such that, so that
>**ob** whether, if

Continued

1 **Er wird uns Bescheid sagen können, nachdem er angerufen hat**
   Nachdem er angerufen hat, wird er uns Bescheid sagen können
   He will be able to let us know for certain, once he has phoned

2 **Wenn ich ins Kino gehe ...**
   When(ever) I go to the cinema ...
   Ich komme, wenn du willst
   I'll come if you like

3 **Es regnete, als ich in Köln ankam**
   Als ich in Köln ankam, regnete es
   It was raining when I arrived in Cologne

4 **Er möchte wissen, wann der Zug ankommt**
   He would like to know when the train is due to arrive

5 **Während seine Frau die Koffer auspackte, bereitete er das Abendessen zu**
   Er bereitete das Abendessen zu, während seine Frau die Koffer auspackte
   He made the supper while his wife unpacked the cases

6 **Ich warte, bis du zurückkommst**
   I'll wait till you get back

7 **Da er nicht kommen wollte, ...**
   Since he didn't want to come ...

8 **Wir haben den Hund nicht mitgenommen, damit im Auto genug Platz war**
   Damit im Auto genug Platz war, haben wir den Hund nicht mitgenommen
   We left the dog at home so that there would be enough room in the car

Word Order: Main Clauses

● In a main clause the subject comes first and is followed by the verb, as in English:

His mother (*subject*) drinks (*verb*) whisky (**→1**)

● If the verb is in a compound or passive tense, the auxiliary follows the subject and the past participle or infinitive goes to the end of the clause (**→2**)

● The verb is the second concept in a main clause. The first concept may be a word, phrase or clause (**→3**)

● Any reflexive pronoun *follows* the main verb in simple tenses and the auxiliary in compound tenses (**→4**)

● The order for articles, adjectives and nouns is as in English: "a/the/this/that" + *adjective(s)* + *noun* (**→5**)

● A direct object usually follows an indirect, except where the direct object is a personal pronoun.
But the indirect object can be placed last for emphasis, providing it is not a pronoun (**→6**)

● The position of adverbial expressions (see p.188) is not fixed. As a general rule they are placed close to the words to which they refer. Adverbial items of *time* often come first in the clause, but this is flexible (**→7**)
Adverbials of *place* can be placed at the beginning of a clause when emphasis is required (**→8**)
Adverbial items of manner are more likely to be within the clause, close to the word to which they refer (**→9**)

● Where there is more than one adverb, a useful rule of thumb is "time, manner, place" (**→10**)

Continued

1 Seine Mutter trinkt Whisky
His mother drinks whisky

2 Sie wird dir etwas sagen She will tell you something
Sie hat mir nichts gesagt She told me nothing
Es ist für ihn gekauft worden It was bought for him

	1	2
Die neuen Waren	**kommen**	**morgen**
The new goods	are coming	tomorrow

	1	2
Was du gesagt hast,	**stimmt**	**nicht**
What you said	isn't true	

4 Er rasierte sich He shaved
Er hat sich rasiert He (has) shaved

5 ein alter Mann an old man
diese alten Sachen these old things

6 Ich gab dem Mann das Geld I gave the man the money
Ich gab ihm das Geld I gave him the money
Ich gab es ihm I gave him it/I gave it to him
Ich gab es dem Mann I gave it to the man
Er gab das Geld seiner Schwester
He gave the money to his sister (*not his brother*)

7 Gestern gingen wir ins Theater } We went to the theatre
Wir gingen gestern ins Theater } yesterday

8 Dort haben sie Fußball gespielt } They played football
Sie haben dort Fußball gespielt } there

9 Sie spielen gut Fußball They play football well
Das war furchtbar teuer It was terribly expensive

10 Sie haben gestern furchtbar schlecht dort gespielt
They played dreadfully badly there yesterday

Word Order: Main Clauses (ctd.)

- A pronoun object precedes all adverbs (→**1**)
- While the main verb must normally remain the second concept, the first concept need not always be the subject. Main clauses can begin with many things, including:
  - an adverb (→**2**)
  - a direct or indirect object (→**3**)
  - an infinitive phrase (→**4**)
  - a complement (→**5**)
  - a past participle (→**6**)
  - a prepositional phrase (→**7**)
  - a clause acting as the object of the verb (→**8**)
  - a subordinate clause (→**9**)
- If the subject does not begin a main clause, the verb and subject must be turned around or "inverted" (→**2-9**)
- Beginning a sentence with something other than the subject is frequent in German.

  It may however also be used for special effect to:
  - *highlight* whatever is placed first in the clause (→**10**)
  - *emphasize* the subject of the clause by forcing it from its initial position to the end of the clause (→**11**)
- After inversion, any reflexive pronoun precedes the subject, unless the subject is a pronoun (→**12**)
- The following do not cause inversion when placed at the beginning of a main clause, although inversion may be caused by something else placed after them:
  - **und, allein, oder, sondern, denn** (→**13**)
  - **ja** and **nein** (→**14**)
  - certain exclamations: **ach, also, nun** *etc* (→**15**)
  - words or phrases qualifying the subject: **nur, sogar, auch** *etc* (→**16**)

1 Sie haben es gestern sehr billig gekauft
They bought it very cheaply yesterday

2 Gestern sind wir ins Theater gegangen
We went to the theatre yesterday

3 So ein Kind habe ich noch nie gesehen!
I've never seen such a child!
Seinen Freunden wollte er aber nicht helfen
He wouldn't help his friends

4 Seinen Freunden zu helfen, hat er nicht versucht
He didn't try to help his friends

5 Deine Schwester war es It was your sister

6 Geraucht hatte er nie He had never smoked

7 In diesem Haus ist Mozart auf die Welt gekommen
Mozart was born in this house

8 Was mit ihm los war, haben wir nicht herausgefunden
We never discovered what was wrong with him

9 Nachdem ich ihn gesehen hatte, ging ich nach Hause
I went home after seeing him

10 Dem würde ich nichts sagen! I wouldn't tell *him* anything

11 An der Ecke stand eine riesengroße Fabrik
A huge factory stood on the corner

12 Daran erinnerten sich die Zeugen nicht
The witnesses didn't remember that
Daran erinnerten sie sich nicht They didn't remember that

13 Peter ging nach Hause, und Elsa blieb auf der Party
Peter went home and Elsa stayed at the party
BUT **Peter ging nach Hause, und unterwegs sah er Kurt**
Peter went home and on the way he saw Kurt

14 Nein, ich will nicht No, I don't want to
BUT **Nein, das tue ich nicht** No I won't do that

15 Also, wir fahren nach Hamburg So we'll go to Hamburg
BUT **Also, nach Hamburg wollt ihr fahren**
So you want to go to Hamburg

16 Nur seine Mutter wollte es ihm nicht glauben
Only his mother wouldn't believe him
BUT **Sogar mit dem Zug ginge es nicht schneller**
It would be no faster even by train

Word Order: Subordinate Clauses

- A subordinate clause may be introduced by:
  a relative pronoun (see p.174) (→**1**)
  a subordinating conjunction (see p.222) (→**2-3**)

- The subject follows the opening conjunction or relative pronoun — **wir** and **er** in examples **1-3**

- The main verb almost always goes to the end of a subordinate clause (→**1-3**)

  The exceptions to this are:

  1. in a **wenn** clause where **wenn** is omitted (see p.64) (→**4**)
  2. in an indirect statement without **daß** (see p. 64) (→**5**)

- The order for articles, nouns, adjectives, adverbs, direct and indirect objects is the same as for main clauses (see p. 224), but they are all placed between the subject of the clause and the verb (→**6**)

- If the subject of a reflexive verb in a subordinate clause is a pronoun, the order is *subject pronoun + reflexive pronoun* (→**7**) If the subject is a noun, the reflexive pronoun may follow or precede it (→**8**)

- Where one subordinate clause lies inside another, both still obey the order rule for subordinate clauses (→**9**)

1 **Die Kinder, die wir gesehen haben ...**
   The children whom we saw ...

2 **Da er nicht schwimmen wollte, ist er nicht mitgekommen**
   As he didn't want to swim he didn't come

3 **Ich weiß, daß er zur Zeit in London wohnt**
   I know he's living in London at the moment
   Ich weiß nicht, ob er kommt
   I don't know if he's coming

4 **Findest du meine Uhr, so ruf mich bitte an**
   (= **Wenn du meine Uhr findest, ruf mich bitte an**)
   If you find my watch, please give me a ring

5 **Er meint, er werde es innerhalb einer Stunde schaffen**
   (= **Er meint, daß er es innerhalb einer Stunde schaffen werde**)
   He thinks (that) he would manage it inside an hour

6 *main clause:*
   Er ist gestern mit seiner Mutter in die Stadt gefahren
   He went to town with his mother yesterday
   subordinate clauses:
   Da er gestern mit seiner Mutter in die Stadt gefahren ist ...
   Since he went to town with his mother yesterday ...
   Der Junge, der gestern mit seiner Mutter in die Stadt gefahren ist ...
   The boy who went to town with his mother yesterday ...
   Ich weiß, daß er gestern mit seiner Mutter in die Stadt gefahren ist
   I know that he went to town with his mother yesterday

7 **Weil er sich nicht setzen wollte ...**
   Because he wouldn't sit down ...

8 **Weil das das Kind sich nicht setzen wollte, ...**
   OR: **Weil sich das Kind nicht setzen wollte, ...**
   because the child wouldn't sit down

9 **Er wußte, daß der Mann, mit dem er früher gesprochen hatte, bei einer Baufirma arbeitete**
   He knew that the man he had been speaking to earlier worked for a construction company

Word Order (ctd.)

In The Imperative

- normal order (→**1**)
- with reflexive verbs (→**2**)
- with separable verbs (→**3**)
- with separable reflexive verbs (→**4**)

In Direct and Indirect speech

- the verb of saying ("he replied/he said") must be inverted if it is placed within a quotation (→**5**)
- the position of the verb in indirect speech depends on whether or not **daß** (see p.66) is used (→**6**)

Verbs with Separable Prefixes (see p.72 to 75)

- in main clauses the verb and prefix are separated in simple tenses and imperative forms (→**7**)
- for compound tenses of main clauses and all tenses of subordinate clauses, the verb and its prefix are united at the end of the clause (→**8**)
- in a present infinitive phrase (see p.46), the verb and prefix are joined together by **zu** and placed at the end of the phrase (→**9**)

1 **Hol mir das Buch!** (*singular*)
    Holt mir das Buch! (*plural*) } Fetch me that book!
    Holen Sie mir das Buch! (*polite*)

2 **Wasch dich Sofort!** Wash yourself at once!
    Wascht euch Sofort! Wash yourselves at once!
    Waschen Sie sich sofort! (*polite*)

3 **Hör jetzt auf!** (*singular*)
    Hört jetzt auf! (*plural*) } Stop it!
    Hören Sie jetzt auf! (*polite*)

4 **Dreh dich um!** (*singular*)
    Dreht euch um! (*plural*) } Turn round!
    Drehen Sie sich um! (*polite*)

5 **"Meine Mutter" sagte er, "kommt erst morgen an"**
    "My mother," he said, "won't arrive till tomorrow"

6 **Er sagte, daß sie erst am nächsten Tag ankomme**
    He said that she would not arrive until the next day
    Er sagte, sie komme erst am nächsten Tag an
    He said she would not arrive until the next day

7 **Er machte die Tür zu** He closed the door
    Ich räume zuerst auf I'll clean up first
    Hol mich um 7 ab! Pick me up at 7 o'clock!

8 **Er hat die Tür zugemacht** He closed the door
    Ich werde zuerst aufräumen I'll clean up first
    Er wurde um 7 abgeholt He was picked up at 7
    Wenn du mich um 7 abholst, ... If you pick me up at 7
    Nachdem du mich abgeholt hast, ...
    After you've picked me up

9 **Um frühzeitig anzukommen, fuhren wir sofort ab**
    In order to arrive early we left immediately

Question Forms

Direct Questions

- In German, a direct question is formed by simply inverting the verb and subject (→1)

- In compound tenses (see pp.22ff), the past participle or infinitive goes to the end of the clause (→2)

- A statement can be made into a question by the addition of **nicht, nicht wahr** or **doch**, as with "isn't it" in English (→3)
  Questions formed in this way normally expect the answer to be "yes".

- When a question is put in the negative, **doch** can be used to answer it more positively than **ja** (→4)

Questions Formed Using Interrogative Words

- When questions are formed with **interrogative adverbs**, the subject and verb are inverted (→5)

- When questions are formed with **interrogative pronouns** and **adjectives** (see p.144 and 176 to 178), the word order is that of direct statements:
  1. as the subject of the verb at the beginning of the clause they do not cause inversion (→6)
  2. if *not* the subject of the verb *and* at the beginning of the clause they do cause inversion (→7)

Indirect Questions

These are questions following verbs of asking and wondering *etc.* The verb comes at the end of an indirect question (→8)

1 **Magst du ihn?**
Do you like him?
Gehst du ins Kino?
Do you go to the cinema? Are you going to the cinema?

2 **Hast du ihn gesehen?**
Did you see him? Have you seen him?
Wird sie mit ihm kommen?
Will she come with him?

3 **Das stimmt, nicht (wahr)?** That's true, isn't it?
Das schaffst du doch? You'll manage, won't you?

4 **Glaubst du mir nicht? — Doch!**
Don't you believe me? — Yes I do!

5 **Wann ist er gekommen?** When did he come?
Wo willst du hin? Where are you off to?

6 **Wer hat das gemacht?** Who did this?

7 **Wem hast du es geschenkt?** Who did you give it to?

8 **Er fragte, ob du mitkommen wolltest**
He asked if you wanted to come
Er möchte wissen, warum du nicht gekommen bist
He would like to know why you didn't come

Negatives

A statement or question is made negative by adding:

> **nicht** (*not*) or **nie** (*never*)

- The negative may be placed next to the phrase or word to which it refers. The negative meaning can be shifted from one element of the sentence to another in this way (→**1**)

- **nie** can be placed at the beginning of a sentence for added emphasis, in which case subject-verb inversion occurs (→**2**)

- **nicht** comes at the end of a negative imperative, except when the verb is separable, in which case **nicht** *precedes* the separable prefix (→**3**)

- The combination **nicht ein** is usually replaced by forms of **kein** (see p.126) (→**4**)

- **doch** (see p.196) is used in place of **ja** to contradict a negative statement (→**5**)

- Negative comparison is made with **nicht ... sondern** (*not ... but*). This construction is used to correct a previous false impression or idea (→**6**)

1 Er wollte mit ihr nicht sprechen
He didn't want to speak to *her*
Er wollte nicht mit ihr sprechen
He didn't *want* to speak to her

Er will nicht morgen nach Hause
He doesn't want to go home *tomorrow*
Er will morgen nicht nach Hause
He doesn't want to go *home* tomorrow

Wohnen Sie nicht in Dortmund?
Don't you live in Dortmund?
Warum ist er nicht mitgekommen?
Why didn't he come with you?
Waren Sie nie in Dortmund?
Have you never been to Dortmund?

2 Nie war sie glücklicher gewesen
She had never been happier

3 Iß das nicht! Don't eat that!
Beeilen Sie sich nicht! Don't hurry!
BUT **Geh nicht weg!** Don't go away!

4 Gibt es keine Plätzchen? Aren't there any biscuits?
Kein einziges Kind hatte die Arbeit geschrieben
Not a single child had done the work

5 Du kommst nicht mit. — Doch, ich komme mit
You're not coming. — Yes I am

6 Nicht Peter, sondern sein Bruder war es
It wasn't Peter, but his brother

Numbers

Cardinal (one, two etc.)	**Ordinal** (first, second etc)	
null	**0**		
eins	1	der erste[2]	1.
zwei[1]	2	der zweite	2.
drei	3	der dritte	3.
vier	4	der vierte	4.
fünf	5	der fünfte	5.
sechs	6	der sechste	6.
sieben	7	der siebte	7.
acht	8	der achte	8.
neun	9	der neunte	9.
zehn	10	der zehnte	10.
elf	11	der elfte	11.
zwölf	12	der zwölfte	12.
dreizehn	13	der dreizehnte	13.
vierzehn	14	der vierzehnte	14.
fünfzehn	15	der fünfzehnte	15.
sechzehn	16	der sechzehnte	16.
siebzehn	17	der siebzehnte	17.
achtzehn	18	der achtzehnte	18.
neunzehn	19	der neunzehnte	19.
zwanzig	20	der zwanzigste	20.
einundzwanzig	21	der einundzwanzigste	21.
zweiundzwanzig[1]	22	der zweiundzwanzigste[1]	22.
dreißig	30	der dreißigste	30.
vierzig	40	der vierzigste	40.

1. zwo often replaces zwei in speech, to distinguish it clearly from drei : zwo, zwoundzwanzig etc.

2. The ordinal number and the preceding definite article (and adjective if there is one) are declined e.g.:
   sie ist die zehnte she's the tenth
   bei seinem dritten Versuch at his third attempt

fünfzig	50	der fünfzigste	50.
sechzig	60	der sechzigste	60.
siebzig	70	der siebzigste	70.
achtzig	80	der achtzigste	80.
neunzig	90	der neunzigste	90.
hundert	*a hundred*	der hundertste	100.
einhundert	*one hundred*		
hunderteins	101	der hunderterste	101.
hundertzwei	102	der hundertzweite	102.
hunderteinundzwanzig	121	der hunderteinundzwanzigste	121.
zweihundert	200	der zweihundertste	200.
tausend	*a thousand*	der tausendste	1000.
eintausend	*one thousand*		
tausendeins	1001	der tausenderste	1001.
zweitausend	2000	der zweitausendste	2000.
hunderttausend	100 000	der hunderttausendste	100 000.
eine Million	1 000 000	der millionste	1 000 000.

- With large numbers, spaces or full stops are used where English uses a comma e.g.:
  1.000.000 or 1 000 000 for 1,000,000 (*a million*).

- Decimals are written with a comma instead of a full stop e.g.:
  7,5 (**siebenkommafünf**) for 7.5 (*seven point five*).

Fractions

halb	half (a)
die Hälfte	half (the)
eine halbe Stunde	half an hour
das Drittel	third
das Viertel	quarter
zwei Drittel	two thirds
dreiviertel	three quarters
anderthalb/eineinhalb	one and a half
zweieinhalb	two and a half

Time

Wie spät ist es?	What time is it?
Wieviel Uhr ist es?	
Es ist ...	It's ...

00.00	**Mitternacht / null Uhr / vierundzwanzig Uhr / zwölf Uhr**
00.10	**zehn (Minuten) nach zwölf / null Uhr zehn**
00.15	**Viertel nach zwölf / null Uhr fünfzehn**
00.30	**halb eins / null Uhr dreißig**
00.40	**zwanzig (Minuten) vor eins / null Uhr vierzig**
00.45	**viertel vor eins / dreiviertel eins / null Uhr fünfundvierzig**
01.00	**ein Uhr**
01.10	**zehn (Minuten) nach eins / ein Uhr zehn**
01.15	**Viertel nach eins / ein Uhr fünfzehn**
01.30	**halb zwei / ein Uhr dreißig**
01.40	**zwanzig (Minuten) vor zwei / ein Uhr vierzig**
01.45	**viertel vor zwei / dreiviertel zwei / ein Uhr fünfundvierzig**
01.50	**zehn (Minuten) vor zwei / ein Uhr fünfzig**
12.00	**zwölf Uhr**
12.30	**halb eins / zwölf Uhr dreißig**
13.00	**ein Uhr/ dreizehn Uhr**
16.30	**halb fünf / sechzehn Uhr dreißig**
22.00	**zehn Uhr / zweiundzwanzig Uhr / zwoundzwanzig Uhr**

morgen um halb drei	at half past two tomorrow
um drei Uhr (nachmittags)	at three (p.m.)
kurz vor zehn Uhr	just before ten
gegen vier Uhr (nachmittags)	towards four (in the afternoon)
erst um halb neun	not until half past eight
ab neun Uhr	from nine o'clock onwards
morgen früh/abend	tomorrow morning/evening

The Calendar

Dates

Der wievielte ist heute?	What's the date today?
Welches Datum haben wir heute?	

Heute ist ...	It's ...
der zwanzigste März	the twentieth of March
der Zwanzigste	the twentieth

Heute haben wir ...	It's ...
den zwanzigsten März	the twentieth of March
den Zwanzigsten	the twentieth

Am wievielten findet es statt?	When does it take place?
Es findet am ersten April statt	... on the first of April
Es findet am Ersten statt	... on the first
Es findet (am) Montag, den ersten April, statt	
Es findet Montag, den 1. April, statt	
It takes place on Monday, the first of April/April 1st	

Years

(im Jahre) 1984 (neunzehnhundertvierundachtzig) in 1984
Er wurde 1970 (neunzehnhundertsiebzig) geboren
He was born in 1970

Other Expressions

im Dezember/Januar *etc* in December/January *etc*
im Winter/Sommer/Herbst/Frühling
in winter/summer/autumn/spring
Anfang September at the beginning of September
nächstes Jahr next year

Punctuation

German punctuation differs from English in the following cases:

Commas

- Decimal places are always shown by a comma (→**1**)

- Large numbers are separated off by means of a space or a full stop (→**2**)

- Subordinate clauses are always marked off from the rest of the sentence by a comma (→**3**)
  This applies to all types of subordinate clause e.g.:

  clauses with an adverbial function (→**3**)

  relative clauses (→**4**)

  clauses containing indirect speech (→**5**)

- A comma is not required between two main clauses linked by a co-ordinating conjunction (→**6**)

Exclamation Marks

- An exclamation mark is occasionally used after the name at the beginning of a letter, but this tends to be rather old fashioned (→**7**)

- Exclamation marks are used after imperative forms unless these are not intended as commands (→**8**)

1 3,4 (dreikommavier) 3.4 (three point four)

2 20 000 OR **20.000 (zwanzigtausend)**
20,000 (twenty thousand)

3 Als er nach Hause kam, war sie schon weg
She had already gone when he came home
Er bleibt gesund, obwohl er zuviel trinkt
He stays healthy, even though he drinks too much

4 Der Mann, mit dem sie verheiratet ist, soll sehr reich sein
The man she is married to is said to be very rich

5 Er sagt, es gefällt ihm nicht
He says he doesn't like it

6 Ich möchte hin aber ich darf nicht
I would love to go but I can't

7 Liebe Elke! ... Dear Elke, ...
Sehr geehrter Herr Braun! ... Dear Mr. Brown, ...

8 Steh auf! Get up
Bitte, nehmen Sie doch Platz
Do please sit down

The following index lists comprehensively both grammatical terms and key words in German and English contained in this book.